Beardi
Avia
1913 -

The story of a Scottish industrial giant's aviation activities

By

©Charles E. Mac Kay

Beardmore Inverness N184 is lowered onto the Clyde

Front cover: Stuart Culley prepares for his first flight in the Beardmore built Sopwith 2F-1 Camel, N6812, July 1918

Beardmore Aviation

1913 – 1930

The story of a Scottish industrial giant's aviation activities

By

Charles E. Mac Kay

© Charles E. Mac Kay

Bristol Puma Trainer first used at Renfrew 1923

Published and graphic design by

A. MacKay

G12 0DY

Printed by Clydeside Press, 37 High Street, Glasgow, G1 1LX   Editor: Iain C. MacKay

ISBN 978-0-9573443-0-3   First published: 2012

This text is copyright. All rights reserved. No part of this publication may be reproduced, copied, edited, modified or stored in a retrieval system, hard drive, or transmitted in any form, electronically or by any other means, including letter or review, without prior written permission from the author, family heritor's or publisher.

William Beardmore, 1st Baron Invernairn (16 October 1856–9 April 1936). Sponsor of the 1907 Antarctic Expedition and arms manufacturer, Owner of Flichity House, Perth.

A.S.N Gritton

Patrick Cogan

For my children, Angus,
Graham, Charles and Michelle Caroline

CONTENTS

ACKNOWLEDGEMENTS — Page 6

PREFACE — Page 8

OH HAPPY BAND OF PILGRIMS — Page 10
Harwich Force and Beardmore Camel N6812

William Beardmore & Co Ltd — Page 14
How the company was formed in Scotland
How Dalmuir became centre of aviation manufacture

AEROPLANES — Page 35
The pre - war DFW aeroplanes
Aeroplanes built during the Great War at Dalmuir
Post – war research into Rohrbach metal aeroplanes
The last aeroplanes built at Dalmuir

AERO – ENGINES — Page 117
The Austro-Daimler series at Arrol Johnston
The evolution of the BHP at Galloway Motors
The airship engines at Parkhead
Loss of airship R101

AIRSHIPS — Page 166
How the company became involved in airships
Building airships at Inchinnan
A short history of each airship

H. M. S. ARGUS — Page 183
Evolution of the aircraft carrier
Testing H.M.S. Argus, Chanak Crisis
Deployment to China, Squadrons on board
The Second World War

Beardmore School of Reserve Flying — Page 207
Setting up the school
Aircraft at Renfrew
Some accidents, administration and closure

Appendices with Bibliography — Page 217

ACKNOWLEDGEMENTS

Grateful acknowledgements are made to the following for assistance in research and for comments on the manuscript during preparation of the text: Mrs A. Ramsay, my reading tutor and Squadron Leader R.D.C. Gibson D.F.C.*, J.P. (R.A.F.Rtd.) publisher and friend; Neil B. Morris of H. Morris &Co. Ltd (The Morris furniture Group) guide and friend; Alma Topen, manager G.U.A. Business Records, James Nixon, Vana Skelley; Michael Moss and the staff of the Glasgow University Archive; The Librarian and staff Social Sciences, Science and Technology, History and Topography, the Glasgow Room of The Mitchell Library, Glasgow;
The Aviation Bookshop London for supplying assistance and information.; Michael Evans Rolls-Royce Heritage Trust; The Secretary S.B.A.C.; Peter Elliot Librarian Royal Air Force Museum; Publicity Department, Castrol (U.K.); Sqdn.Ldr. Singleton R.A.F. (Rtd.), R.C.M. King and E.A. Munday (now retired) of the Air Historic Branch Ministry of Defence; F. H. Lake for J. C. Andrews, Chief Librarian, Whitehall Library, M. O. D.; The Librarian and Secretary, Royal Aeronautical Society; Andrew Nahum, Science Museum London; Keeper of the Exhibits, Imperial War Museum; the Curator, Royal Scottish Museum of Flight, East Fortune; Carroll Johnston of British Aerospace Kingston; The Archivist, Messerschmitt - Bolkow - Blohm; John S. Goddin, Public Relations Manager, British Aerospace Military Aircraft Division and to Mike Stroud. Emrys Inker of J. & G. Weir P. L. C.; David Charleton of British Aerospace Bristol; Peter Clegg; George Brown R.A.F. Rtd.; the Archivist and staff Strathclyde Regional Archives; Chaz Bowyer and Robert Mellichamp U.S.A.; H. J. Woodend, Custodian and Staff of the M. O. D. Pattern Room; Caledonia Models; the Manager, Tom Dickson Cameras, Byres Road, Glasgow; Mr Ayub, Your Price, Partick, Glasgow; Jonathan Nicholson, Civil Aviation Authority; the Librarian and Staff of Bishopbriggs Library; W.H.Wallace, Librarian, V. S. E. L.; M.D. Richardson, Fleet Air Arm Museum; Michael Bragg for research at the Public Records Office; I am also grateful to my friends for listening to me during the life of the project and unwittingly guiding me through the journey. I am deeply indebted to

the Great War aviation historian, J. M. Bruce for assistance and support during the preparation of the text and for his comments on the accuracy of the manuscript; John Hood, District Chief Librarian, Pat Malcolm and Kay Lelane for their assistance at Clydebank District Libraries & Museum Department. I am also grateful to my family for the support they gave me during the recommencement and reconstruction of the text and encouraging me to complete the project. I have been given fullest access to surviving company papers, documents, files etc. I alone am responsible for the views, conclusions and statements expressed.

Charles E. Mac Kay

Preface

This book concentrates on the aviation activities of the Glasgow firm of William Beardmore & Co. Ltd. It is not meant to be a definitive history or claim to be anything but a history. It is intended as a short work, or guide, which looks at the growth of the aircraft industry in Clydeside and Scotland during the Great War and beyond to 1930, though the history of H.M.S. Argus takes it to 1946. The root of the project arose out of an interest in misidentification of aircraft and from this simple aim the work took off. There was very little to go on at first, for I found that I was working in fresh territory and there was no single key source to refer to. The company did produce a history of aircraft production just after the war but the archive copy disappeared and this book is meant to complement it.

There is a family involvement with Beardmore. My grandfather worked for the firm at Parkhead from 1907 to 1934 where he was an iron moulder, journeyman/patternmaker. When I was five, I sat on his lap and he would say, with a twinkle in his eye, "William Beardmore took my lungs." From him I learned it was not the First World War but "The Great War." He sat in front of the fire and it was there, on that same chair, that my great uncle Patrick wept his eyes out in the autumn of 1917, wondering if he would ever return from the front – he did not. My mother testified to this often.

This study took place when there was no internet, no public domain and no pdf, or for that matter, PCs with word processors or e-mail or mobile phones. Before the text was constructed, a lot of research took place, firstly at the University of Glasgow Business Records, secondly at the Mitchell Library Glasgow and thirdly from my own reference books and knowledge. The many firms that once had aviation departments, or the various ministries of the government ably assisted me. In some cases, enquiries were forwarded to other parties and I was very surprised that there was a response. Of course, there was a great pooling of information with other researchers.

All references to place names are contemporary. If there was only one reference found it would only be used if there was another confirming reference. Such was the case for Renfrew Aerodrome and the Dalmuir airfield. I am grateful to all the institutions for granting me access to their records and the time they gave me. My friend Jack

Bruce guided me through the manufacturers and pointed me in the right direction. My other friend Mike Bragg was working on his mighty tome on radar at the time. When he was at the Public Records Office, he put together contract numbers and totals from the records of the Ministry of Munitions and other sources. We both felt that these tables would be an important aid to the researcher or reader in the future. We were both surprised to find that the records of the Ministry of Munitions were nearly 100% complete. For clarity, all tables are within a chapter and not in a separate appendix. I also felt it would be good to work in the area of government departments. The Great War changed the life of Britain. For the first time in British history, government went right into the complete life of the individual from the cradle to the grave and we are still living with this today. The work of these departments during this war was outstanding.

The text was first written by hand from note. It was re- read a few times then it literally was cut and pasted. Small slivers of paper were glued to a fresh piece of paper and edited. Once this was done, it was re – read and typed up on a typewriter. The hardest part was finding a shape to the book. I felt it was easier to do the company, then the aircraft, the aero-engines, the airships, Argus and then the flying school with the appendix. The bibliography was included in the appendix. Very little has been written about Rohrbach, so this is included in the appendix along with other relevant company information. Much is included which is from local tradition and that has been included because, "Ne prorsus interent" – "lest they perish altogether." The majority of the images are from my own collection, now defunct companies, the family collection, or the collection of J.M.Bruce and Chaz Bowyer and are all used with permission.

As time went by the Apple Mac became available and the text was then transferred to the word processing bundle in the Apple Mac, initially an LCII and finally to an LC475. The software was Claris Works, which was easy to use. Claris was utilised to Claris Works 5/Apple Works 5. Then versions were brought out that were PC compatible, these were Claris 3 and then Claris 5. From the latter the work was transferred to Word 97 and then all its versions, working in a Windows environment. Finally, the work was saved as a pdf.

"Oh Happy Band of Pilgrims"
Harwich Force and Beardmore Camel N6812

This war was just over four years old and both sides were at an impasse. There had been deadlock on the Western Front since 1914 and an indecisive naval action at the Battle of Jutland in 1916. On 21st March 1918, the Germans had tried to destroy the British Army in the field and had failed. They had tried exactly the same tactics with France at Verdun in 1915. In this fourth year of war, the tenacity of the British soldier had rescued the French on the Marne and the Italians against the Austrians. The British had even mounted a seaborne operation at Zeebrugge with daring and élan in the spring of 1918. By 8th August 1918, the Germans were being out generalled and outfought on the Franco-Belgian battlefield. Today was the 11th August 1918, ten past six in the morning and Rear Admiral Tyrwhitt was worried about his situation, because he was about to set a trap.

There was a report of German airships in his area and Harwich Force, his command, was out hunting and was heading across the North Sea to the island of Helligoland. Their prey was a huge Zeppelin that had shadowed the British fleet some ten days earlier. Today three destroyers were with Harwich Force towing flying boats mounted on lighters, but with the complete absence of wind and the presence of swell, it would be impossible to get them into the air. A fourth destroyer, H.M.S. Redoubt, was towing a lighter with a Sopwith Camel on board. As arranged, at ten past seven, three flying boats from Yarmouth arrived. When they arrived, Harwich Force and the Admiralty commenced strong signal traffic. The flying boats then went off to patrol the area, but because of the fog, they did not notice German seaplanes in the vicinity. The flying boats returned to Harwich Force an hour later. They were then instructed to go and search for some coastal motor boats that Harwich Force had sent out earlier. During the progress of their search, the flying boats noticed a patrolling Zeppelin. Once again, they flew back and reported to Rear Admiral Tyrwhitt, by visual signal, the presence of the huge airship.

At the same time as the flying boats were signalling Tyrwhitt the Admiralty informed him of the presence of the Zeppelin - the trap was set. Harwich Force then turned to seaward making smoke. At nearly 19000 feet, the Zeppelin L53 was perfectly positioned over the British fleet and as far as her captain, Kapitanleutenant Prolls was concerned, no British aircraft could attack him at this altitude. Little did he realise he was wrong. Aboard the Camel lighter, eighteen-year-old Stuart Culley climbed into the cockpit of his single seat Sopwith 2F-1 ship's aeroplane, serialled N6812. Redoubt towed the lighter at thirty knots and on her thirty foot planked deck the Camel was prepared for flight. At 8.41 am, after a run of less than five feet, N6812 was airborne, climbing rapidly and headed for L53. Due to the presence of the fog, the crew of the Zeppelin did not notice the tiny aeroplane until after nine thirty, but by then it was too late. At 18700 feet, Culley attacked head on from below with his twin Lewis Guns. He fired seven rounds of incendiary from his number one gun into the airship's envelope and then it jammed. Lifting the nose of the Camel higher, Culley fired a full drum of incendiary from his number two Lewis into the L53.

Losing engine power, he pushed the control column forward putting the nose down. Just then, the Zeppelin burst into flame and L53 fell into the North Sea a mass of burning fabric, flaming gas and molten metal. The falling debris was clearly visible to ships over fifty miles away. That same bad visibility which had helped Stuart Culley now worked against him and for two hours he flew around in the fog trying to find his attendant destroyer. At last he found H.M.S. Redoubt and he put the Camel down in the sea beside the lighter. When the aeroplane was hoisted on board, it was found that only one pint of petrol was left in the tank. So successful was the recovery that "Culley's Camel" was soon flying again. Jubilant, Rear-Admiral Tyrwhitt signalled his ships as follows: - "Flag general - Your attention is drawn to Hymn No 224 Verse 2." And to those who looked, it said:-

> "Oh happy band of pilgrims,
> Look upward to the skies
> Where such a light affliction
> Shall win so great a prize."

Sopwith 2F-1 Camel, N6812 was manufactured in July 1918 at Dalmuir Naval Construction Works, Scotland, by William Beardmore & Co., Ltd. and is preserved to this day at the Imperial War Museum, South Lambeth, London

.

H.M.S. Redoubt   Zeppelin L53

Rear-Admiral Tyrwhitt

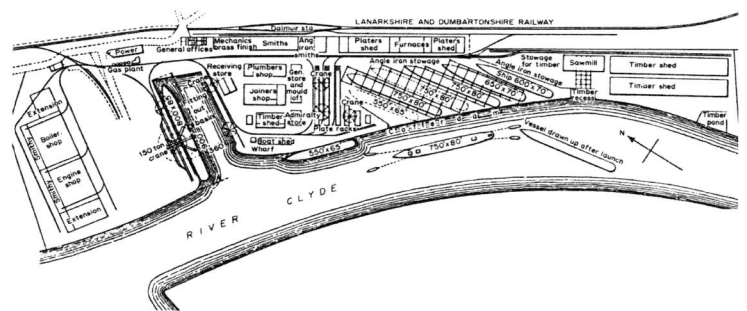

The Beardmore shipyard river frontage about 1904

The Dalmuir shipbuilding gantry with "The Twa Bobs," man and horse centre

William Beardmore & Co.Ltd
How the company was formed in Scotland
How Dalmuir became centre of aviation manufacture

The Glasgow firm of William Beardmore & Co., Ltd has its roots in the world's oldest marine engineering firm of Robert Napier & Son of Glasgow. It was in 1861 that Robert Napier, the father of Clyde shipbuilding and heavy engineering, invited William Beardmore from England to Scotland. His purpose was to form a partnership with his son-in-law, William Rigby, at the Parkhead Forge, which was on the outskirts of Glasgow's east end. Napier had sold the Parkhead Forge to Rigby in 1860. After the partnership had been formed all went well until 1863 when William Rigby suddenly died, but the Rigby connection did not end there, because Mrs Rigby became Beardmore's partner. Evidently, the terms of the new partnership did not suit Mrs Rigby and, after seven years, she left the business.

In 1877, William Beardmore, senior, died and his son, also called William, took over the firm. The burden of such a complex organisation was too much for William Beardmore and he invited his uncle Isaac Beardmore to the Parkhead Forge to help run the business. This partnership was a success and by 1899, through effective management and control, the Parkhead Forge became the largest iron and steel complex of its kind in the country.

As a means of diversification, William Beardmore branched out into shipbuilding, taking out the lease to Napier's Govan shipyard. In a way, this was a wise move, since shipbuilding required large amounts of steel and iron for production and Beardmore had the capacity and volume at Parkhead to cover this demand. In 1901, William Beardmore decided to move his shipbuilding operation from Govan to the old Clyde Navigation Trust's maintenance workshops at Dalmuir. Earlier, in 1899, this part of the Clyde river frontage had been bought by William Beardmore replacing the interest of James Shearer & Sons of Scotstoun. Later this move was seen as a joint Vickers - Beardmore move to halt the expansion of Beardmore's major competitor, John Brown. Problems with cash flow meant that William Beardmore had to merge with the Vickers concern in 1906, a move that William Beardmore used to his advantage.

William Beardmore & Co., Ltd had specifically set up the Dalmuir Naval Construction Works to attract Admiralty orders for the new battleship programme. This programme centred on the production of a new turbine battleship called, "Dreadnought", but the order that Dalmuir received was for one of the last pre-Dreadnoughts, H.M.S. Agamemnon. To add insult to injury, Agamemnon's turret armament of 12" guns had been procured for the name ship of this new class, H.M.S. Dreadnought. Orders for new battleships were slow and William Beardmore now applied his philosophy of total personal involvement in his business to back his financial empire and get orders. He employed the services of the Polar explorer Ernest Shackleton at Parkhead in a capacity that has still yet to be determined, (Shackleton travelled daily from Edinburgh to Parkhead to carry out his duties.) Beardmore also subsidised his expeditions to Antarctica. This involvement with Ernest Shackleton gave William Beardmore membership of the Royal Yacht Squadron and access to people of influence and it also gave that great glacier in Antarctica a name - Beardmore. From the Admiralty came Captain Onyon as a manager of ordnance at Dalmuir and from the Allan Line came Colonel J. Smith Park who became a Director, resulting in orders for liners. Axel Bremberg became the firm's gun designer resulting in a whole series of ordnance from 37 m.m. to 15 inch calibre being manufactured at Parkhead and Dalmuir.

Two further battleships H.M.S. Conqueror and H.M.S. Benbow were added to H.M.S. Agamemnon and later still came the Royal Sovereign Class Battleship, H.M.S. Ramillies. The Alan Line ordered the passenger liner Alsatian, which was finished in 1914 and was regarded as one of the finest vessels then built on the Clyde. William Beardmore bought an interest in the Italian Line of Lloyd Sabuado of Genoa and this too resulted in further orders for ships.

In 1913, heavy ordnance was laid down at Parkhead Forge manufacturing plant, but was immediately mothballed. Although the international situation was tense, no one could really perceive war as it was to come. Clearly, there was a pre - war arms race and William Beardmore & Co. Ltd. was clearly in the running looking for orders. With warships and heavy armaments came the newest weapon - aeroplanes.

On 13th May 1912, the British Government formed the Royal Flying Corps (R. F. C.) with a Military Wing and a Naval Wing. The War Office administered the Military Wing while the Naval Wing came under the authority of the Admiralty. This Admiralty move into aeronautics was purely financial, since the Admiralty wanted to expand their cash flow that the War Office had earlier succeeded in obtaining from the government. The Admiralty to back its interest in aviation set up its own Air Department in September 1912 with Commodore Murray F. Seuter as its head.

By November 1913 William Beardmore & Co. Ltd., moved into aviation when they decided to enter into the production of aeroplanes, airships and aero - engines. The aero - engines were to be manufactured at the Arrol-Johnston works at Heathfield in the Scottish Borders. This firm was wholly owned by William Beardmore and not a corporate part of the Parkhead-Dalmuir operation. The aeroplanes were to be built in England as Beardmore - D.F.W.s under the management of the Austrian, E. C. Kny, while the airships were to be the concern of the Dalmuir works. Aviation had attracted the interest of another of the company Directors, the Marquis of Graham. In 1912, he designed what would now be called an aircraft carrier, but the Admiralty had rejected the design because of insufficient experience had been built up by the Royal Navy with aeroplanes at sea.

In July 1914 the Admiralty wrested control of its air arm from joint War Office control and set up the Royal Naval Air Service, (R.N.A.S.) A month later, on Tuesday 4th August 1914, Britain declared war on Germany and the long - expected war broke out. The Admiralty were decisive. They halted all capital ship work in order to conserve armour plate capacity. Parkhead was to concentrate on the manufacture of ordnance and armour plate, while Dalmuir diversified into aviation, ordnance, warships and, latterly, tanks. With the new defence regulations introduced when the war began, E. C. Kny was interned on the Isle of Man, his only payment from Beardmore being commission of nineteen pounds for the building of a "Round Britain Seaplane."

At Dalmuir, an airfield was laid out between Old Kilpatrick and the Corporation of Glasgow's sewage treatment works, a spur railway and the River Clyde. The airfield was constructed to test fly production and prototype aircraft before they were delivered to the R.N.A.S. and later the R.F.C. The firm employed the services of a test pilot A. D. "Ducky" Jones, who had been a test pilot for Flanders aircraft. He commenced flying at the airfield in the spring of 1915. He had been with Beardmore - D.F.W. at Brooklands in the autumn of 1914. With aircraft development, came Admiralty orders and in August came the first order for aeroplanes. In this instance, it was the Royal Aircraft Factory B. E.2c.

   As each order came in, Beardmore allocated a contract number, additional spares and one - off prototypes were allocated a further Admiralty job number. Unfortunately, Dalmuir did not have the necessary production facilities and the first aeroplanes were manufactured in the Cabinet Makers Shop or in the Mechanic's Shop. The first aeroplanes were made by the mechanics of the Paisley firm of Messrs' Fullarton, Hodgart and Barclay, who were at Dalmuir on Admiralty sub - contract work. They promptly went on strike for an additional 2d an hour on top of their basic wage, only going back to work ten days later in September. As each aeroplane was completed, it was taken along to the airfield minus its wings, the wings were then fitted and the machine was test flown by A.D.Jones. Airship construction was a more difficult proposition for the shipyard and the early design, planning and expertise came from Beardmore's partner - Vickers.

   Other arms manufacturers had moved into aviation at the same time as William Beardmore & Co. Ltd. Vickers had started with airships at Barrow in 1913, while Armstrong - Whitworth opened up its own aircraft department in 1914. But such was the shortage of arms capacity in Britain, that early in 1915 the government set up its own arms agency - the Ministry of Munitions, under the former Chancellor of the Exchequer, Lloyd George. The existence of this organisation was to have a profound effect on the running and outcome of the war. All over Britain, the country was divided up into munitions districts, each district with its own munitions committee. Glasgow and the West of Scotland were regarded as an Admiralty district with its own organisation. Admiral Johnston Stewart and his assistant, Captain Brian Bartellot, were the local Admiralty representatives with their headquarters at Clyde View in Partick, Glasgow. Since Beardmore was regarded as an Admiralty contractor, they were not allowed to accept aircraft orders from the War Office. However, in the case of the Nieuport XII they were allowed to proceed with a batch of aircraft. As a means of control at Dalmuir, the Admiralty posted in its own representative Lieutenant G.T. Richards who was commissioned into the Royal Naval Volunteer Reserve (R.N.V.R.) in the autumn of 1914. G.T. Richards was originally from Manchester and before the war had worked for Rolls - Royce as a draughtsman. Leaving that firm, he had set up business as a consultant engineer and designer and formed a partnership with Cedric Lee. Together they designed a circular aeroplane, but the design failed, as did their partnership, around 1913. Even though the Admiralty employed him, G.T. Richards still designed and patented his own aircraft designs out with his own duties at Dalmuir. The Construction Branch of the Admiralty ordered aircraft at Dalmuir. They also issued contracts for airships and kite balloons with the contractor. The Acceptance Organiser of the Aeroplane and Seaplane Construction Branch, Admiralty, was made responsible for all new types of aeroplanes completed at Dalmuir. Initially these duties were the responsibility of Lieutenant G. T. Richards, but in September 1915 the Admiralty Air Department was re-organised with a new Director of Air Services, Admiral Vaughn Lee and with this new phase came a change in the Beardmore organisation.

William Beardmore had decided that his firm should now move into the aeroplane manufacturing business, with Dalmuir being the centre of this operation. A design office was set up in January 1916 with some of the staff from the firm's naval architect side. One of the new team was James Dickson who had been involved in the design phase of S. S. Alsatian and the Italian Liner Conte Rosso. Lieutenant Richards was allowed to resign his commission in December 1915 to set up this new department. A purpose built aviation shed for building aeroplanes was erected near the banks of the Clyde and used for aeroplane and airship manufacture, but the shed was only completed in 1918 due to shortages of wartime building materials. This meant that the majority of aeroplanes, built at Dalmuir during the Great War, were manufactured in the original cabinetmakers and joiner's shops of 1914.

Aeroplanes of those times were built around wood, fabric and wire, materials well used in the shipyard. The Admiralty supplied aeroplane timber for both air services, the R.N.A.S. and R.F.C. The timber used was chiefly silver spruce and its substitutes, walnut, ash, poplar, mahogany, and other hardwoods. Beardmore also manufactured aircraft propellers and the only suitable wood for this application was black American Walnut, but because of shortages, laminates of mahogany and walnut were used instead. This method of using laminates of scrap pieces of wood came later in the war and was called the "Oddy and Cleaver Method." Dalmuir manufactured propellers for Britain's first aero - engine, the Green engine, the swivel propellers for the Vickers Airship R 23, the Bentley B.R. 2 and all the aeroplanes built at Dalmuir.

BE2c and Wight seaplanes under construction 1915

BE2cs under construction

WB V centre, Sopwith Camels and SB III under construction 1918

Wight Seaplanes in the foreground with BE2cs

Wight 840 Seaplane 1400 under construction 1915 with BE2c background

Airship R34 and Handley Page V/1500, Inchinnan, 1918

Dalmuir seaplane sheds, top right, were not completed till after the war

Sopwith Beardmore just being finished at Dalmuir

A.D. Jones with G.T Richards and WB1

Sir William Weir D.G.A.P.

Beardmore Sopwith, 2F-1 Camel, which served aboard H.M.S. Undaunted.

WILLIAM **BEARDMORE** & Co. Ltd.
STEEL MANUFACTURERS,
SHIPBUILDERS & ENGINEERS
GLASGOW & DALMUIR.

Again, the Admiralty supplied another important manufacturing product and that was aeroplane fabric. Vickers built the Ioco works at Anniesland, in the west end of Glasgow and the fabric manufactured there was used for airships as well as aeroplanes.

In aircraft, the fabric used was a two - ply rubberised fabric. On the airships the outer cover, including the fin, used a single ply, doped and varnished. Because of the greater air pressure at the nose the bow used the stronger two-ply grade. To strengthen the fabric for flight and to make it stretch across the aeroplane structure it had to be treated with cellulose dope. Vickers had an interest in "The British Cellulose and Chemical Manufacturing Company" formed by them with a Swiss firm, the "Cellonite Company." This company helped overcome the shortage of dope at an early stage in the war. For William Beardmore the creation of this company was a windfall. He received more than half the shares of the Vickers interest in the company. Parkhead also supplied the Admiralty with steel tubing and the company declared that they had supplied 80% of the wartime capacity for aeroplane construction. At this stage in the war, the drain in manpower was enormous. The battlefields of France, the Royal Navy and the Ministry of Munitions were all making demands for labour. Skilled manpower was in short supply and the Government had to resort to desperate measures. Women were to be introduced as a matter of policy; this policy was called "Dilution."

Dilution had been introduced to release skilled workers from war service into more skilled production methods such as tool - making. This policy struck at the everyday life of the worker, his job, his security and ultimately his pay - the only solution the workers could see, even in the middle of a war, was to go on strike. The Ministry of Munitions had also issued their famous circular L2 which aimed at a policy of equal pay for women, with women earning one pound a week guaranteed minimum wage. This added more confusion to an already tense situation. Enough was enough and the men went on strike in March of 1916, but by 14th June, agreement had been reached on Clydeside for the introduction of women workers throughout the heavy engineering and munitions industry. As early, as 1st January 1916 women had been introduced to aeroplane manufacture at Dalmuir and one of their duties was to stretch the fabric over the aeroplane structure. Their overseer in this case was Lieutenant Brown. Due to demarcation disputes with the unions, refugee workers from the continent were engaged in aeroplane work. As a member of the Vickers group, who had sponsored the Belgian refugee workers, Beardmore introduced Belgians into the sheet metal shop. Their supervisor was Mr Zohrab. Although these arrangements were met with hostility by the unions, by the end of August 1916 final agreement was reached between the unions and the employers for the introduction of Dilution and the use of refugees in manufacturing. Belgian refugees were housed in Glasgow and the families received ten shillings a week subsistence allowance from the Belgian Refugee Committee. Royal Navy officers who were posted to such places as

Dalmuir came under the authority of the Assistant - Superintendent of Construction. Since initially Beardmore designs were experimental G. T. Richards did not liaise with the Superintendent of Construction, but with the Assistant Superintendent of Design. For the first two years of the war, the Admiralty gave the orders for aeroplanes, airships and kite balloons, while officers of the Admiralty Air Department were supervising final assembly. Then, towards the end of 1916, came another change in policy. In early 1915 aeroplane construction, on a sub - contract basis, commenced on Clydeside. The firm who ran this scheme were J. & G. Weir of Cathcart and their Managing Director, William Weir, had suggested in May 1916 that aeroplane supply should be transferred to the Ministry of Munitions. Evidently, his idea was a good one, for on 1st March 1917, transfer of all aeronautical supply from the War Office and Admiralty, to the Ministry of Munitions, took place. The new Director General of Aircraft Production in the Ministry of Munitions was William Weir.

The Ministry of Munitions took over the existing War Office departments, which supplied aeroplanes to the R. F. C. Most of the War Office's branches continued under new names, but absorbed the staff of the Admiralty. Beardmore functions were only slightly altered by this new arrangement since the Ministry adopted Admiralty policy for design, which relied heavily on the design staffs of private firms. During 1917, the Ministry of Munitions installed their own Production Officer at Dalmuir, under the authority of the Supply and Production Department, Ministry of Munitions. As the war progressed, his duties involved obtaining materials, watching progress, making suggestions to design work, working out contracts and patent fees, directing labour and implementing Dilution as a matter of policy. With the change of agency for the air services there then came a change in ordering spares. The Admiralty policy of ordering aircraft spares as a separate contract was abandoned, spares were now ordered as one seventh of the total aircraft contract. This included wings, fuselages, tail planes etc. One of the discussion points between G. T. Richards and the Production Officer were aircraft power plants. Beardmore had taken over the production rights to a small steam turbine which Richards thought could be adapted to aeroplanes, but when the plans were received from Weirs it was found that the boiler would be approximately the size of the aircraft (the Handley Page V/1500). The plans were shelved.

The Ministry of Munitions Production Officer oversaw the construction of the Sopwith Pup, S. B. 3d, Wight 840, Nieuport XII and the prototypes of the W. B. II, W. B. IV and V. He followed up orders such as those for the Sopwith Camel and Handley Page V/1500. Only the airships came under full Admiralty control. In their case final production and assembly was undertaken not at Dalmuir, but at Inchinnan, which is across the River Clyde. At this stage in the war, the aeroplane was now seen as having reached its true wartime role. It could break the deadlock in the trenches, strike at the German navy and bring the war to the German capital, Berlin. The British aircraft manufacturers were now in a strong position to influence government and they formed the Society of British Aircraft Constructors (S.B.A.C.) with William Beardmore & Co., Ltd., as a founder member. Since the Germans had bombed London in July 1917, the government formed a committee under General Smuts to look at the running of the air services. Because of his recommendations, it was decided to amalgamate the R. N. A. S. and the R. F. C. to form the Royal Air Force (R. A. F.) with an Independent Air Force. To strike at Germany a new bomber was ordered - the Handley Page V/1500, for the Independent Air Force under General Trenchard.

The coming of the Armistice in November 1918 brought the liquidation of contracts, the ending of controls from the Ministry of Munitions and the ending of Dilution, with the women being paid off by 31st December 1918. The Belgian workers returned home as soon as possible and by the spring of 1919 they had all but left the West of Scotland. Dalmuir as a munitions centre was deeply involved in the post - war euphoria. As a means of diversification, the Ministry of Munitions, as a matter of policy, designated Beardmore at Dalmuir as a centre for steam locomotive manufacture, but there was a problem. Dalmuir still had an Aviation Department. With less than six hundred aeroplanes manufactured at Dalmuir, all of other aircraft designs, but with its own design department, William Beardmore & Co., Ltd., in 1918 was in a remarkably stable financial position. This was probably due to guaranteed cash - flow from the government, rather than

William Beardmore's control of the operational side of the company. In early 1919 the Beardmore Aviation Department manufactured a batch of body panels for Beardmore Taxis because they had not yet received any aircraft orders. Liquidation of the aircraft contracts for the Sopwith Camel and V/1500 continued, together with some airship work.

The Air Ministry, set up during the war to administer Civil and Military aviation, started a series of competitions for aircraft. G. T. Richards designed two competition machines the W. B. IX and W.B. X. As a means of increasing aerial awareness among the public it was decided to subsidise and start airmail services around the country. For this scheme, Dalmuir completed two aeroplanes based on an earlier design, the W. B. IIb. Between 1919 and May 1920, G. T. Richards designed the following aeroplanes: -

A. The W. B. IIa Fighter reconnaissance biplane, which was projected only.
B. The W. B. VI a six passenger-folding aeroplane of 500 H.P., which was powered by the Galloway Atlantic. Construction started, but the machine was not completed.
C. The W. B. VI b two seat folding aeroplane with either the 160 H.P. or the 230 H.P. B.H.P. This was projected only.
D. The W. B. VIc single seat folding aeroplane with either the 40-50 H.P. A. B. C. Projected only.
E. The W.B. VId six passenger folding aeroplane with two fuselage installed 230 H.P. B.H.P. engines, driving two propellers, through shafts and belts. Projected only.
F. The W.B. VIII, a 24-passenger aeroplane, with three 500 H.P. Galloway Atlantics that was projected only.

Illustrating the company's confusion of the times, plans were released for another W. B. VI. In this case, it was a torpedo bomber, which was very similar to the Sopwith Cuckoo. All these designs came to nothing. Surplus ex - bombers such as the D. H. 9 were being sold off in quantity and were being used as transports throughout the country and there was no demand for new build aircraft. Clearly, this was a situation where the directors or his managers were not advising William Beardmore properly.

WILLIAM BEARDMORE & CO. LTD.
Naval Construction Works · DALMUIR

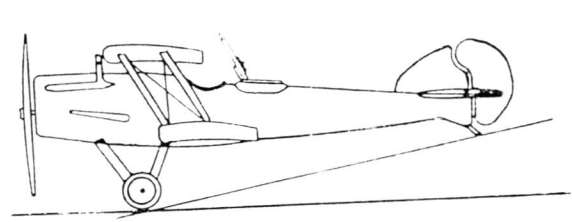

Projected W.B.IIa 1918-1921

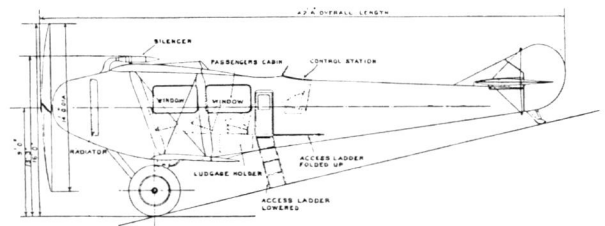

Projected W.B.VIa 1918-1919

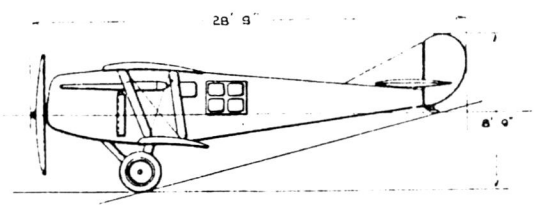

Projected W.B.VIb 1918-1919

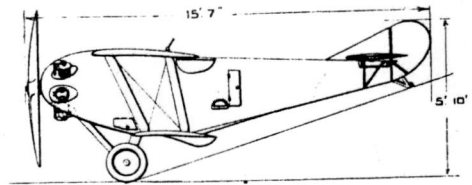

Projected W.BVIc 1919

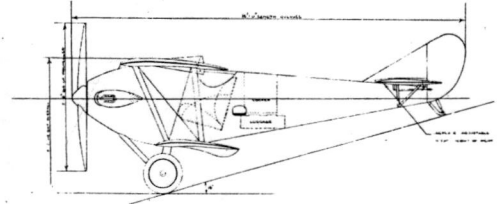

Second projected W.BVIc 1919 note engine

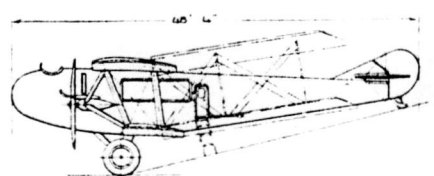

Projected W.BVId 1919

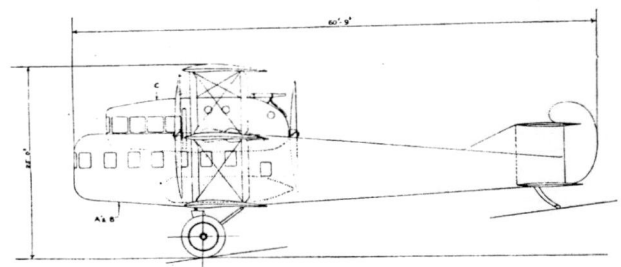

Projected W.BVIII 1919

None of the post-war activities in the aviation field met with any success. After a meeting of the Directors at Dalmuir, the only one ever held there by the Beardmore organisation, the Beardmore Aviation Department closed down in May 1920. G.T. Richards was paid off with a bonus of £150 and he immediately moved south to become General Manager of Martinsyde Aircraft. When this firm closed down Richards tried to develop and improve the typewriter and, from this, he went to the Science Museum, cataloguing the museums aero - engine collection and becoming their scientific lecturer.
Unfortunately, for the firm's first designer, E. C. Kny, the regulations had forbidden any payments to enemy aliens during the war and post Armistice years, but in 1922, when he was declared bankrupt, he at last received fifteen hundred pounds for the work he carried out at Brooklands for Beardmore - D.F.W in 1914.

Between 1920 and 1922, there was little movement at Dalmuir for the production of aeroplanes. Small one - off projects such as torpedo gear and metal propellers were manufactured, but there was little activity from the Air Ministry to encourage orders.
The Air Ministry then approached aeroplane companies, which were members of the S. B. A. C. The Royal Air Force had plans for expanding its reserve and at the heart of the scheme was an idea to retrain wartime pilots for the newly formed Reserve Air Force. Ultimately, these reserve officers were to form the backbone of the newly planned Territorial Air Force - the Auxiliary Air Force. At Renfrew, the company set up a flying school to retrain these officers. With the expansion in personnel came the desire for experimental machines. In 1923 Dalmuir received orders for all - metal aircraft which were to be built for the Air Ministry. With the reopening of aircraft manufacture, Beardmore decided to re- enter the manufacturing side on its own account.

W. S. Shackleton was appointed as the firm's designer and he started work at Dalmuir on 1st January 1924. Shackleton went on to design two aeroplanes for William Beardmore, the W.B. XXIV and the W.B. XXVI. There were other orders for aircraft and the Air Ministry wanted tests on all-metal aircraft ordering three all-metal aeroplanes. The all - metal aircraft were to be German in origin and used Rohrbach patents in their designs. Rohrbach had passed all their plans and technical information on these aircraft to the Beardmore Company. The first Beardmore all - metal aircraft was delivered on 18th September 1925. This was an Inverness flying boat, with the other two aircraft being delivered in the period 1928 - 1929. For Shackleton, working at Dalmuir must have been very unhealthy, for his health broke down and he left the firm to move to Australia. Squadron Leader Rollo de Haga Haig, as outside manager, took Shackleton's place.

Rollo De Haga Haig was a test pilot at Farnborough and had flown autogiros there. He had completed fighter trials with the R33 airship and flew the Boulton - Paul twin engined machine in public displays. He was also a member of the Haig family, which included the former Commander in Chief of the British Army in France, Earl Haig. Another new member of the team was the Swiss engineer, H. J. Steiger. Together they tried to improve the Rohrbach flying boat's design detail, but they never designed any new Beardmore aeroplanes. Steiger had seen the potential of the Rohrbach wing design and with de Haga Haig patented a new aircraft wing called the Mono - Spar. Thurstan James, former editor of "The Aeroplane," also worked at Dalmuir before moving to Shorts in 1926. However, by March 1928, things were not at all well financially with the Beardmore Empire.

The banks saw the financial state of the whole company as jeopardising their interests, even with the Air Ministry work at the flying school and the experimental orders for aircraft at Dalmuir. The banks were looking for a scheme to reconstruct the firm. For many years, William Beardmore & Co., Ltd. had depended for its survival on its relationship with Vickers, but in June 1926 this Vickers arrangement had been ended and there was no independent life - line to save the company. A joint Managing Director was appointed with William Beardmore. This was Lewis Craven Ord, formerly of Armstrong Whitworth. He took up his appointment at the company headquarters, Parkhead, on 13th June 1928. While the company was going through dramatic financial difficulties, William Beardmore managed to obtain a £28000 loan at 4%, from the company. At a meeting of the board of directors, on 16th October 1928, Ord broke the news that the Air Ministry had closed the flying school. The Directors then agreed that aircraft work, carried out at Dalmuir, was to be excluded from the company's operation and that Ord was to make the arrangement. William Beardmore & Co. Ltd. resigned its membership from the S. B. A. C. on 30th January 1929, with Dalmuir closing down its aviation side in February 1929. Tragically, for William Beardmore, he had to resign as a Director from his own firm in September 1929 and the following month came the Stock Market Crash.

H. J. Steiger, together with de Haga Haig, left Beardmore and then formed the Monospar Aircraft Company. De Haga Haig found the finance for the infant aircraft company through his friendship with M. L. Bromson, a banker. Their first Monospar aircraft flew on 27th February 1931, at the same time as the stock of the Dalmuir Aircraft Department was sold for scrap. This aeroplane was G - ABUZ and was registered to C. Hayward, a director of Mono spar and an old Beardmore employee. Soon General Aircraft took over Monospar with H. J. Steiger becoming their chief designer. This company became part of the Blackburn Group, but none of their aircraft used the mono- spar wing system in their designs.

Dalmuir was never to build any ships or aircraft again. Shipbuilding was closed down and the site used by Beardmore Diesels up to 1936. They continued to buy and supply diesel engines as an agency until 1941. In 1939, the company was involved with SMT in the production of aircraft wings at Airdrie. During the war years, the site was used as a Royal Ordnance Factory and was heavily damaged during the Clydebank Blitz of March 1941.

William Beardmore did not live to see the war clouds rise over Clydeside; he died at his home, Flichity House, Strathnairn, on 9th April 1936 and was buried in the grounds of his estate. Isaac Beardmore died just before him and is buried in Glasgow's Eastern Necropolis, behind the Cathedral of Saint Mungo.

While sailing on his converted trawler near Plymouth, on 10th November 1936, Rollo De Haga Haig fell over the side of his boat and his body was never recovered. Twelve years later on the 21st September 1948, E.C.Kny died at the age of 61 in Germany. He had left aviation to go on to design a range of electrical road vehicles at Leipzig. H. J. Steiger returned to Clydeside becoming General Manager at Blackburn of Dumbarton just before the outbreak of the Second World War, managing this concern through the war years and into the nineteen fifties when Major Bumpus replaced him. Today at Dalmuir, nothing but memories and ghosts remain to indicate the site of the Dalmuir Naval Construction Works and the work of the Aviation Department of William Beardmore & Co., Ltd.

Adolf C. Rohrbach

Rollo de Haga Haig

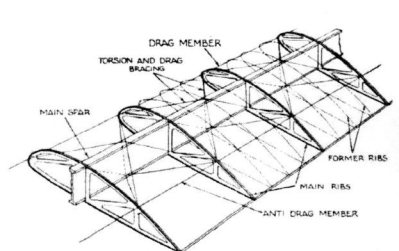

The Steiger mono - spar wing

General Aircraft Monospar ST-4 mk1

Aeroplanes

The pre - war DFW aeroplanes
Aeroplanes built during the Great War at Dalmuir
Post – war research into Rohrbach metal aeroplanes
The last aeroplanes built at Dalmuir

D. F. W.

In late 1913, William Beardmore & Co., Ltd. took over the building rights in this country of the German Aircraft Works, Deutsche Flugzeug Werke (D. F. W.) of Liendenthal near Leipzig. Up to November 1913, this company had been known as Mars and their aircraft had been successfully used in the Balkan Wars. At the D.F.W. Works the Technical director was E. C. Kny, an Austrian, and he had a staff of 56 engineers with 722 workers. Kny was also an aircraft designer and is credited with designing, around 1909, an early form of wing flap. Kny was a frequent visitor to the United Kingdom and in 1912 had entered a monoplane in the Military Aircraft Trials, but this aeroplane was withdrawn at the insistence of the German Government. D.F.W. then set up business at Brooklands and in November 1913 Kny brought over from Germany two examples of the D. F. W. Biplane. These aircraft were described as the D. F. W. Military Biplane type B2 and a D.F.W. Arrow Biplane. They had two pilots. One was Oskar Roemplar while the other was A.D.Jones.

In the Military Biplane, the fuselage was built up of three tubular longerons connected by a system of three-ply wooden cross – members. The engine, a 100 H.P. Mercedes, was mounted on ash beams. The lower fuselage was formed by steel wires running longitudinally and supported on the cross - members to form a streamline shape. The fuselage behind the pilot was made of three-ply wood giving it a "turtle - back." The B2 had a crew of two, sitting in tandem, with the pilot at the rear towards the tail. The pilot had a large wheel at the top of the control column that operated the ailerons, while the rudder was controlled by a foot bar. In the front cockpit was a duplicate set of controls, which could easily be removed giving the

D.F.W. Military Biplane the possibility of two roles, Scout and Trainer. Between the crew was a 50-gallon fuel tank, which gave an endurance of seven and a half hours, supplemented with a four-gallon tank under the upper wing. The wings were constructed of ash spars with poplar side pieces, over which were built the ribs of three-ply wood. For ease of storage the wing - tips could be folded. The weight of the D. F. W. was 1460 lbs., with a climb rate of 300 ft. per minute and a maximum speed of 68 M.P.H.

The B2 was demonstrated at Brooklands in a blaze of publicity in January 1914, where it was flown in front of the press by Oskar Roemplar in a flight of twenty minutes duration. By February 1914 it was being tested at Farnborough by the War Office, where it displayed very good flying characteristics. At the end of the trial, the B2 was flown back to Brooklands by Herr Roemplar to join the other D.F.W.

The second D.F.W. was to have been the subject of the licence agreement between Beardmore and Deutsche Flugzeug Werke. E. C. Kny had decided that this machine was to be built in the U.K., not at Dalmuir, but at a purpose built factory at Richmond in Surrey, England. This D.F.W. carried its crew in tandem and power was provided by the 100 H.P. Mercedes engine, with the radiator being mounted on the starboard fuselage side. The fuselage was built of steel tubing covered with fabric, the struts and longerons being secured with clips and acetylene welding. The undercarriage was supported with steel tubing and had one of the first braking systems on any aeroplane in this country.

During May 1914, Lieutenant C.H. Collet R.M.A., who demonstrated the aircraft's excellent flying characteristics, tested one D.F.W. at Brooklands. Collet had only qualified as a pilot in October 1913 at the Central Flying School and clearly the D.F.W. had proved its worth in such inexperienced hands during the trial. By the summer of 1914, the D.F.W. franchise was under the control of Beardmore, which gave Cecil Kny an enthusiastic boost. He returned to Leipzig and ordered three types of D.F.W. for export to Britain. These were, one of all steel structure, a stable military biplane, and a Scout of the "Arrow" type.

Accompanying Kny to Leipzig was A.D.Jones who had officially joined the Beardmore - D. F. W. concern at Brooklands in June 1914.

By July, "The Glasgow Herald" was reporting that a dozen D.F.W.s were coming to Britain, including seaplanes. At the same time, the "Daily Mail" announced that it was holding an aerial competition, to be flown round the country between the 1st - 15th August. This was the Round Britain Air Race. As a seaplane race, the competitors were to start and finish at Southampton with T. O. M. Sopwith's entry to be number one in the take-off line up. E. C. Kny decided to enter a Beardmore - D. F. W. seaplane and this was to be number two position in the race. From Leipzig, Deutsche Flugzeug Werke announced that an all - steel biplane of their design, powered by a 120 H.P. Austro - Daimler engine had set up a world's altitude record of 26,568 feet. Kny's "Round Britain" machine was very similar to this aircraft and was to be powered by the Beardmore built Austro Daimler aero-engine of 120 H.P. It was to be built of steel tubing with a rectangular fuselage built around four longerons. To these were attached tubular steel struts and cross-members, all secured by welding. The crew of two were carried in an aluminium upper fuselage shaped like a "turtle back" with two cut outs for the crew, while the lower fuselage was of fabric. The "Round Britain Beardmore" weighed 1500 lbs., had an estimated speed of 85 M.P.H. and an endurance of six hours. As a seaplane, floats were fitted to the fuselage, but an undercarriage was available for land use. This was the first aircraft component made by Beardmore at Dalmuir. During early August, it was seen being welded by "Flight's" Brooklands correspondent and was finally viewed on 28th August 1914, when it was sold for £138: 13s: 7d, an engine - less hulk. The war cancelled the race and the aircraft was never given the opportunity to prove itself.

D.F.W. under construction at Leipzig

D.F.W. readied for flight in Germany

D.F.W.B2 as 154 with the R.N.A.S. in England, 1914, pilot C.H. Collet

In the Balkan Wars 1913   C.H. Collet in 154 at Leipzig

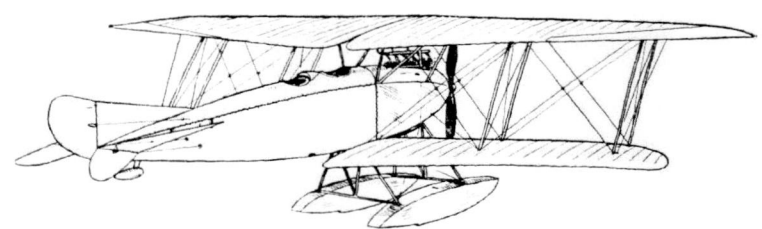

Impression of the round Britain Beardmore – D.F.W. July 1914

The D.F.W.s were mobilised by the Admiralty as 154 and 891 respectively. D.F.W. 154 seeing service before the war began. Under contract no. C.P. 36909/14 it was purchased by the Admiralty and was flown from Portsmouth to Wick by Lieutenant C.H. Collet, with A.D. Jones as a passenger, but because of technical difficulties had to land at Grimsby. Nothing is really known about D.F.W. number 891 except that it was at Killingholme in October 1914 with the other D.F.W., 154. There they were both utilised for daylight patrols where their endurance proved of inestimable value. One flight by 154 has been officially published, for on 18th November 1914, flown by Flight sub-Lt. Adams, DFW 154 left Killingholme at 0730, flew for 40 minutes towards Donna Nook, opposite Spurn Head and landed at Killingholme at 0845.

By the spring of 1915, all D.F.W.s were appearing in the British press as enemy aircraft and the two R.N.A.S. machines were grounded. Lieutenant Collet's D.F.W. 154 was struck off charge in February 1915, but nothing is known concerning the fate of the other machine. As for Lieutenant Collet, his experience with the Beardmore - D.F.W. proved invaluable. On 23rd September 1914, while stationed in Belgium, he made the first ever-bombing raid on German soil. He flew to Dusseldorf and dive - bombed the Zeppelin shed from 400 feet, damaging the shed and the incumbent airship with three bombs. For his bravery Flight Lieutenant C. H. Collet, R. M. A. received the D. S. O. and was the pathfinder for a later generation of Royal Air Force wartime aviators.

Specifications
Military Biplane Type B2 (January 1914)
Engine: 100 H.P. Mercedes.   **Dimensions:** Span 56' (Top), 40' (Bottom)
Max. Speed 68 M.P.H. **Crew:** 2. Weight 1460 lbs. (empty).
[154 in R.N.A.S. service later reported as a D.F.W. Arrow.]

Beardmore - D.F.W.
Round Britain Racer
Engine: 120 H.P. Beardmore - Austro - Daimler. **Dimensions**: Span 44'
Length: 25', Area of main planes: 450 square feet. **Max. Speed:** 85 M.P.H.
Crew: 2 **Weight:** 1500 lbs. [empty]
[All data above estimated, machine not completed.]

D.F.W. Military Biplane (August 1914)
Engine: 100 H.P. Mercedes **Dimensions**: Span 46', Length 27' 6".
Max. Speed: 75 M.P.H. **Crew:** 2
[891 in R.N.A.S. service]

W.B. 1

During 1916, the Admiralty placed an order for a large two-seat bomber to be built at Dalmuir. At this time in the war the two air services, R.F.C. and R.N.A.S. had adopted two completely different policies for bombing. The R.F.C. felt that the only effective use of the bomber was to attack the enemy in the field, including his lines of supply, while the R.N.A.S. had adopted a completely different outlook. The main target for the R.N.A.S. was the airship and its sheds, while the secondary target was to be the munitions works, which provided guns and their replacements. In the autumn of 1916, the Admiralty approached the French Government to allow them to carry out independent bombing from a base at Luxeuil near Belfort. By October 1916 the Admiralty proposed that 200 machines be stationed in France for bombing the German Zeppelin sheds and lines of communication, such as railways and the munitions factories.

To meet the Admiralty requirement for a bomber [to contract A.S.7123] and with the serial N525, G. T. Richards designed a large three bay biplane around the latest engine then available, the B.H.P. As a two-seat bomber, it had a carefully streamlined fuselage with a large four-wheeled undercarriage. The pilot sat well forward, with the observer near the tail. He communicated with the pilot through a two-way system, just like a ship's telegraph. This bomber was designed to carry six 110-pound bombs, which were aimed by the observer through a sight on the floor. It had a single Lewis machine gun mounted on a ring. Called "The Experimental Bomb Dropper Aircraft", it was given the Beardmore Admiralty Job Number 1097. It was test flown by A.D.Jones at Inchinnan in 1917, before being delivered to Cranwell for erection on 16th May 1917 and flew there for the first time on the 8th June 1917. It was accepted on 23rd August 1917. Problems with the B.H.P. engine meant a change to the 240 H.P. Sunbeam engine, but the machine crashed twice and was written off on 8th October 1917. By this time, it had received a new serial number, B9467 after one of its repairs and was named the W.B. 1.

By the time the W.B. 1 was produced the Admiralty were having second thoughts on operational bombers. The new Handley-Page 0/100 was now available in quantity and one Handley Page with one pilot could carry six times the bomb-load of a W.B.1. There was now no real requirement for a two-seat strategic bomber and the W.B. 1 quietly disappeared

Specification

Type: Two seat bomber
Engine: 230 H.P. B. H.P. or Sunbeam engine|
Armament: 1 Lewis machine gun, 6 X 110 lb. bombs
Speed: 91 M.P.H. at sea level
Dimensions: Span: 61 '6 ", Length: 32' 10", Height: 14' 9"

The WB1 at Inchinnan on its maiden flight, Richards walks away

The designer of the W.B.1 with the aircraft

The W. B.1 shows its ungainly appearance at Inchinnan

W. B. II

The design of this aeroplane can be traced back to the B. E.2c, a type that was being produced in quantity for the R.N.A.S. As a modified design the W.B. II was given the job number 1133 with the contract number A. S. 2864/18 and was a more powerful version of the government designed B. E.2c. Richards had seen some deficiencies in the original design and had sought permission to modify it in his own way, with the pilot and observer's positions being reversed. The observer now sat at the rear with his own machine-gun and the gun mounting had a very unusual design. The Lewis machine gun was mounted at the end of a sort of broomstick affair with the observer seated on a pole that was mounted to the floor on a universal ball-joint. The Lewis gun could be swung and manoeuvred with great agility.

The fuselage was made circular in cross-section and power was supplied by the 200 H.P. Hispano-Suiza engine. The wings of the W.B.II were identical to the B.E.2c. The W.B. II first flew in August 1917 and was sent to Martlesham Heath, England, for trials on 27th September 1917. These trials were not a success and the W.B. II was returned to Dalmuir for modification. It was sent back to Martlesham Heath with a new two-bladed propeller, raised gunners cockpit and an access hatch for the magneto. It was then sent for more trials to the Isle of Grain, the test establishment of the R.N.A.S., but still it was rejected.

The W. B. II did not represent any great advance in design at this stage in the war. It was overshadowed by superior designs such as that of the Bristol Fighter, which was then in quantity production. The W.B. II's engine, the 200 H.P. Hispano, was also in short supply and needed for the S. E. 5 Scout. With the rationalisation of aircraft and engine designs at the Ministry of Munitions, the W.B.II was not ordered into quantity production.

Specification

Type: Two seat fighter
Engine: 200 H.P. Hispano - Suiza
Armament: 2 Vickers machine guns and 1 Lewis
Speed: 120 M.P.H. at sea level
Dimensions: Span 34' 10", Length: 26' 10", Height:

The W.B.II at Dalmuir

The W.B.II being readied for its initial flight at Dalmuir

The W.B.II shows the gunner's position in relation to the pilot at Dalmuir

After modification the W.BII is readied for flight

W.B. III

The W.B. III was a modified form of Sopwith Pup for shipboard use. The Ministry of Munitions regarded its modification as a two - way design, 50% by Sopwith and 50% by Beardmore. It was designated the Sopwith - Beardmore 3d or S. B.3d, with G.T. Richards at Dalmuir being the designer of the one hundred built. There was never any Sopwith - Beardmore 3f, they were all designated S. B. 3d. The S. B. 3d is covered more fully in the Sopwith Pup section.

Specification
Type: Single Seat Fighter
Armament: One Lewis Machine Gun
Speed: 101 M.P.H. at ground level
Dimensions: Span 26' 0", Length 20' 2", Height 8' 1"

The W.B.III, N6100, trundled aboard and stored on H.M.S.Cassandra

W.B.IV

In 1917 the Admiralty raised a design for a new fighter to specification N1a, to be powered by the Hispano Suiza engine of 200 H.P. One of the demands of the specification was that the aeroplane should be built around a buoyancy chamber, with the ability to float. Another demand from the Admiralty was that the aircraft be equipped as an airship destroyer. The Admiralty had become interested in heavy anti - airship cannons and were experimenting with a variety of weapons. One such weapon for the specification was the Puteux 37 mm aircraft cannon designed by the French Puteux Arsenal. The drive behind the cannon was not the Arsenal itself, but Marc Birkigt, the designer of the Hispano Suiza engine. He designed the engine with the cannon installed in the engine block with the barrel firing through the propeller hub.

The W.B.IV was an entirely new design for G.T. Richards. It was a large single - seat fighter, designed for shipboard use, with folding wings armed with a Lewis machine gun on the fuselage left hand side and a Vickers machine gun firing through the propeller. [The Puteux cannon were not available at the time and were still under development.] The most unusual feature of the W.B.IV was the engine installation. The practice in those times was to set the engine in the nose or rear fuselage, but, with this design, the engine was in the centre of the fuselage. The propeller shaft ran under the pilot's seat, passing between his legs, with the radiator above and behind the pilot. Buoyancy chambers were built into the nose and forward fuselage and floats were installed at the lower wing tips. For an aeroplane of those times it offered the pilot the best possible view from the cockpit when landing on the ground, sea or ship's deck. Great trouble was experienced with such a novel design and the Ministry of Munitions was still looking for drawings of the machine well into August 1917. A.D.Jones first flew it in late December 1917 and, by the time it went for its Admiralty trials in the spring of 1918, the wing tip floats had been removed. On a test flight, it landed heavily in the sea, smashed in its buoyancy nose chamber and sank. The W.B.IV was a novel design doomed to failure. In wartime conditions, it would have been impossible to service properly at sea and difficult to manage, due to its size. With the availability of the much simpler 2F-1, Camel the W.B.IV was abandoned.

Specification
Type: Single seat fighter
Engine: 200 H.P. Hispano Suiza
Armament: One Lewis and one Vickers machine gun or 37 mm Cannon Puteux
Speed: 110 M.P.H. at sea level
Dimensions: Span 35' 10", Length 25' 6", Height 9' 0"

The W.B.IV at Inchinnan, the pilot has a superb view from the cockpit

Buoyancy chamber is apparent as is the tadpole shape of the rear fuselage

The W.B.IV being readied for flight and at Dalmuir airfield

Marc Birkigt's 200 h.p. Hispano Suiza aero engine

W.B. V

The W.B.V was a much more conventional aircraft, built to the same specification as the W.B.IV, specification N1a. Intended as an airship destroyer with the Puteux heavy gun armament, the W.B.V had the 200 H.P. Hispano engine situated in the nose. A large two bay biplane with wings that could fold, this fighter had a dropping undercarriage and flotation bags fitted to the lower wing. Due to its conventional structure it flew before the other N1a aeroplane, the W.B.IV, in November 1917 and was accepted at the Isle of Grain on 11th January 1918. The design of the W.B.V was ideal for the 37mm Cannon Puteux, but in the time scale of the W. B.V only one 37mm Canon Puteux was available, possibly two, for test in the autumn of 1917. But these guns were only available in France and no production of the Cannon Puteux had taken place in Britain. Two barrels were available for the gun, a smooth bore and a rifled barrel with an expected firepower of 60 rounds a minute. It was first fired in France on 7th November 1917, but was only cleared for service on 7th September 1918. The gun was never fitted to the W.B.V.

Axel Bremberg had designed with Clifford Halley, a unique anti-airship gun that used a loading and extractor system described as, "Lazy Tongs." The gun was called "The Auto Aircraft Gun". It came in three sizes, but the one that was considered suitable for the W.B.V was a top loader with rounds of one pound and twin triggers either side of the breech and of 37mm calibre. When fired, the whole extracting and loading system moved, resembling a large octopus moving through the water. In such a cramped cockpit as the W.B.V, if it had been fired would have caused more damage to the pilot than the attacking airship! Naturally, the pilots refused to fire it and the idea was dropped. Possibly this gun was considered for the Experimental Gun Carriage Machine which was never completed. This gun was put forward for trials, but after December 1917 nothing more was heard of it apart from some Beardmore publicity. The second prototype W.B.V flew in February 1918 and was fitted with the conventional armament of one Lewis and one Vickers machine gun. The N1a specification did not produce an aeroplane that was any better than the Beardmore built Sopwith 2F-1 Camel. These Beardmore designs utilised engines which were then in short supply and needed for other operational aircraft. Due to these constraints the N1a series of Beardmore built aircraft, the W.B.IV and W.B.V were not proceeded with.

Specification

Type: Single seat fighter
Engine: 200 H.P. Hispano Suiza
Armament: One Bremberg - Halley heavy cannon or 37 mm Canon Puteux or One Vickers and one Lewis machine gun.
Speed: 112 M.P.H. at sea level
Dimensions: Span: 35" 10", Length: 36' 7", Height: 11' 10"

The W.B.V shows its conventional lines

The W.B.V at Dalmuir airfield

The W.B.V with wings folded and armament fitted, Canon Puteux below

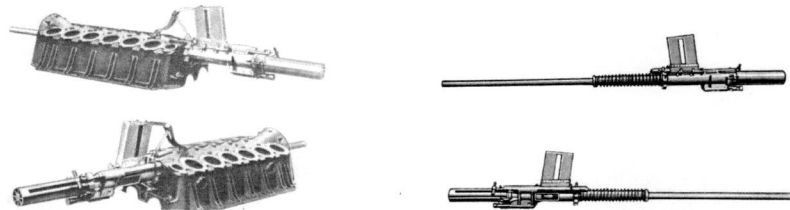

B.E.2c

The Royal Aircraft Factory was founded as a government balloon factory in 1905, then in 1911 it became the Army Aircraft Factory and finally, in 1912, the Royal Aircraft Factory. The factory acted as the technical department for the R.F.C. and then later as technical adviser to the two air services the R.N.A.S. and the R.F.C. The Admiralty little used the aircraft facilities at Farnborough and set up its own technical organisation. Until the end of 1913, the factory was responsible for all the aircraft designs of airships, balloons and aeroplanes used by the R.F.C. The factory came under the control of the Director General of Military Aeronautics, Sir David Henderson. When the war broke out the majority of aeroplanes built by the contractors were to Royal Aircraft Factory designs and the design the contractors based their production on was the B.E.2c.

The design of the B.E.2c can be traced back to 1911 when a Voisin Boxkite, owned by the Duke of Westminster, went to the Army Aircraft Factory for a repair. As a government manufacturer the factory had been banned from manufacturing its own aeroplanes which were in direct competition with those of the private aeroplane manufacturers. The factory was allowed to repair aircraft and the aircraft that was to emerge from the Boxkite repair was the Bleriot Experimental type One or the B.E.1. Surgery and redesign had been carried out by Geoffrey de Havilland and F. M. Green under the pretext of an engine change. The design of the B.E. was progressively updated until it evolved into the B.E.2a of 1912, powered by the 70 H.P. Renault engine. Flown by Geoffrey de Havilland in June 1912, it created a new British altitude record of 10560 ft. It could not qualify for acceptance at the government aircraft trials of that year, but it overshadowed all other designs with the superiority of its performance. Before the outbreak of the war, two revised designs were introduced, the B.E.2A [1913] and the B.E.2b. Both had improved fuel systems, re enforced interplane struts and increased protection for the observer at the front. The B.E.2a [1912] had warping wings, which meant that the wings were twisted to turn, but the design was unstable in flight. The B.E.2b was supposed to be an advance on the original design, but the improvements mentioned above were only a minor modification. Later production B.E. 2s had ailerons instead of wing warping and was produced in large numbers, mostly being powered by the 70 H.P. Renault.

The B.E.2c was built for observation and was the product of Edward Busk's research into stability. Busk had been looking at the flight envelope of the aircraft, including spinning and had made suggestions on how the B.E. series could be modified. The wings were staggered and built with ailerons and the tail was redesigned, making the whole aeroplane inherently stable. This stability, though welcomed by the pilots, made the B.E.2c easy prey in wartime, especially during the time of the "Fokker Scourge." The Fokker was a pioneering monoplane fighter designed for the Germans by the Dutchman, Anthony Fokker. There were few German Fokker monoplanes, but plenty of British B.E.2c targets over the skies of 1915 France. To increase performance the B.E.2c was fitted with the 90 H.P. R.A.F. 1a engine that developed a maximum output of 100 H.P. with 1800 r.p.m. at sea level. In the B.E.2c, the wings were built around wooden ribs and main spars with fabric covering, while the tail was built up in the same manner as the fuselage, wood with fabric covering and wire bracing. The tailskid was of ash on a tubular pylon and the undercarriage was of tubular steel, with a fabric covered spreader bar, while the shock - absorbers were of rubber cord. The fuel tank had a capacity of 26 gallons giving the B.E.2c an endurance of three and a half hours. For the R.N.A.S. and the R.F.C. it performed all general-purpose duties for the first two and half years of the war.

In August 1914 the R.F.C. was made responsible for the aerial defence of this country, but all their aeroplanes were required in France. At the request of Lord Kitchener the Admiralty took over home defence on 3rd September 1914. For these duties, the R.N.A.S. required aeroplanes and the most suitable type then in production was the B.E.2c. In the week of Britain's declaration of war William Beardmore & Co. Ltd attracted an order to build twenty four, B.E.2cs at Dalmuir. This was to be the sixth production batch for this aeroplane in the serial group 1099 – 1122. This order was allocated the Beardmore contract number 524. The contract price negotiated with the Admiralty was £23520 and since the Admiralty regarded the order arrangement the same as that for a ship, the money was paid in instalments, £3525 in 1914 and the whole payment system being paid through appropriation accounts. The first Dalmuir built B.E.2c was flown by A.D.Jones at the firm's airfield on 19th February 1915, some six months after the contract was received. These B.E.2cs had the 70 H.P. Renault engine and the standard Royal Aircraft Factory undercarriage. Order 524 was completed in 1915, giving Beardmore a profit of £8333 : 3s : 6d. Added to this order was a contract to supply twelve B.E.2c fuselages, raising the cost of 524 to £31080. Vickers had been entrusted by the Admiralty to develop an anti - submarine airship, the Submarine Scout Airship, at the express wish of Admiral Fisher. The Submarine Scout Airship or S. S. airships were about 145 feet in length, with a volume of 70000 cubic feet and underneath the gas bag was the fuselage of a B.E.2c. These scouts were the invention of Rear - Admiral Murray Seuter and Commander N. F. Usborne. The first were ordered on 28th February 1915 with the envelopes being supplied by three companies, Shorts, Willows and Airships Ltd, with the first flight taking place on 18th March 1915. With a crew of two, the S. S. series had a maximum speed of 38 M.P.H. and, by the end of the war, 36 S. S. type Scouts had been delivered.

In the summer of 1915, Neville F. Usborne came up with the idea of suspending a complete B.E.2c underneath an airship envelope as an anti - Zeppelin interceptor. As the Zeppelin approached these shores, the B.E.2c was to be cast off, then attack the enemy airship. After preliminary trials in August 1915, another trial was projected for February 1916. On the 21st of that month the B.E.2c which was carrying Usborne as pilot and Ireland as observer was released prematurely. It crashed killing Usborne and Ireland. Three days earlier Usborne's wife had dreamt of an accident and waking him had told her husband of her premonition, but Usborne ignored the fates and died in front of members of the Cabinet who had wanted to see the results of the trial.

8720 first flew May 1916 and was then delivered to East Fortune

Unidentified at Great Yarmouth 1916

8719 went to East Fortune in 1916

Submarine Scout airship, note the envelope and B.E.2c fuselage

Submarine Scout at East Freugh, Scotland, 1918

1099, an early B.E.2c, crashed Whitley Bay, Dec.1915

8724 possibly at Montrose, May 1916, fatal crash Edinburgh Nov.1917

During 1915, Britain and France sent an expedition to the Dardanelles, that narrow passage of sea leading from the Mediterranean into the Black Sea. An aerial presence, including two R.N.A.S. B.E.2cs, operating with No. 3 Wing at Tevedos, was sent to support the allied invasion. During August 1915 six more B.E.2cs arrived as No. 2 Wing. One of these aircraft was used to bomb the Berlin to Constantinople Railway. The newly delivered B.E.2cs included Beardmore machines, which had been fitted with bomb racks and with the front cockpits faired over to be used as bombers.

Around the British coast B.E.2cs were also used for coastal patrol from such stations as Eastbourne, Hornsea, Great Yarmouth, Port Victoria and Scarborough. B.E.2cs were also used at the training schools of Chingford and Cranwell.

The R.N.A.S. received 337 B.E.2cs, of which Dalmuir supplied 110, consisting of 24 from order 524 and 86 from order 541. The latter order was received in 1915 at a cost of £33840, these being serialled in three batches 8326 to 8337, 8488 to 8500, and 8714 to 8724, all these thirty six machines being powered by the more powerful 90 H.P. R.A.F. engine. This order was carried into 1916, when the Admiralty added another batch of fifty. No serials have ever been traced for this batch of aircraft. Before delivery to the R.N.A.S. the aeroplanes were test flown at Dalmuir airfield, dismantled, then crated and forwarded by rail to their allotted units.

On the night of 24th April 1917 there was an air raid alarm at Dover and the local air station was alerted. A Beardmore B.E.2c, 8337, took off. Modified as a night fighter, it was painted black, with a Lewis machine gun over the top wing and it mounted a searchlight. Shortly after take-off it crashed into the Duke of York's School. Initially it hit the roof and then fell into the courtyard in flames, killing the observer and badly burning the pilot who was dragged clear. The use of this Beardmore built B.E.2c as a night fighter was not unique; in late 1915 twenty had been allocated by the R.N.A.S. for the defence of London, but by 16th February 1916 the R.F.C. had taken back their responsibility for the defence of the United Kingdom. The main enemy was still the Zeppelin airship and the only stable aeroplane in available numbers that they could utilise, as a fighter, was the Royal Aircraft Factory designed B.E.2c. In those days night fighter operations were very primitive, but the B.E.2c could provide a steady gun platform if a Zeppelin approached the coast. Of the eighty - nine night fighting flights carried out by September 1915, twenty aircraft were wrecked or damaged, while eleven pilots were injured, with three fatalities.

Then in 1916 came the B.E.2cs greatest successes. During the nights of 31st March, 3rd September, 24th September, 1st October and the 27th November, the night fighters brought down five Zeppelin airships. Towards the end of the year a Beardmore B.E.2c, 8626, flown by Flight Sub Lieutenant E. L. Pulling brought down the Zeppelin L.21 on the night of the 28th November, bringing the total of airships downed that year to six. For this action Pulling received the D. S. O. Unfortunately Pulling was killed in the same aeroplane, 8626, when the aircraft broke up in the air during aerobatics. Such fiery successes for a much maligned and criticised design became the subject of a lot of controversy.

The Royal Aircraft Factory B.E. 2 series marked a great advance over any aeroplanes then in production in British aeronautics. The later B.E.2c was strong, the design sound and the drawings were complete, which meant that manufacturers new to aviation were able to build aeroplanes when they would not normally have done so. For mass production there was no inherently stable machine of private design available and, as for the engine, the only alternative powerplant was the Green Engine, which was not suitable for military aeroplanes. There was an undercurrent of criticism from the press, the military and in the House of Commons as to the worth of the Royal Aircraft

Factory and its designs, including the B.E.2c. The Final Report of the Committee of Administration of the R.F.C. felt that all the criticisms of the B.E.2c were unfounded. But how were pilots expected to destroy intruders whose altitude was at least 10000' higher than their own aircraft?

Specification

Type: Two seat fighter, bomber or reconnaissance aircraft
Engine: 70 H.P. Renault or 90 H.P. R.A.F.1a
Dimensions: Span 36' 10", Length 27' 3", Height 11' 4"
Endurance: 3.5 hrs.
Note: B.E.2c's and "d's" on order as at 1 March 1917 (For the Ministry of Munitions) = 5

The Wight Seaplane

The seaplanes that existed prior to the outbreak of the Great War were only capable of carrying a small load due to the low power of their engines. The principal weapon of the seaplane was to be the 14" torpedo and this was demonstrated at the Spithead Naval Review in July 1914. The standard torpedo carrying floatplane of the R.N.A.S. was the Short 184, powered by the 225hp Sunbeam engine. Designed to the same specification as the Short, was the Wight 840, which was similar to the Short with twin floats and carried the same 14", 840 lb. torpedo. Though not as aerodynamically sound as the Short, the Wight was powered by the same engine, the 225H.P. Sunbeam. The Wight 840 had a maximum speed of 81 M.P.H. with a loaded weight of 4453 lbs. and carried a crew of two. About seventy aeroplanes of this type were built, with sub - contract production being undertaken by Portholme Aviation and William Beardmore & Co., Ltd.

   What is intriguing about the Beardmore involvement with the Wight 840 is the fact that they built the Wight 840 through their own licence agreement with the parent company and not one arranged by the Admiralty. The licence agreement between Wight and Beardmore was signed at Parkhead on 4th May 1915 and received the yard order number 532. The Admiralty allocated the serials for twelve aeroplanes to this order, 1400 to 1411, costing £31080 to build. The first Wight 840 was lowered into the Clyde, possibly at Old Kilpatrick, on 8th September 1915 and was flown by A.D.Jones. Some of this batch of twelve seems to have been accident prone and unable to stand the rigours of the R.N.A.S. 1403 broke up under tow after a forced landing and 1408 and 1409 were destroyed in premature bomb explosions. Nine Wight 840s served at Dundee, one was on H.M.S. Campania and two were based at Gibraltar. The Admiralty ordered another batch of twenty in 1915 in the serial range 9021 to 9040. Beardmore had allocated the number 539 to this second contract and it cost £48460 to produce. In 1916, another batch of four was manufactured at Dalmuir. These were complete machines and not spares.

Order 539 was modified to Admiralty requirements and when the machines were completed they were test flown on the Clyde, lifted, broken down into kit form, packed in cases and sent to their units. The first six were cased and delivered by rail to Dundee. Two were sent to Gibraltar, while the balance was held as spares. 1405, which was with H.M.S. Campania, survived until February 1916 when it was struck off charge: 9027 and 9028 were struck off charge at Gibraltar in July 1916. While being tested by A.D.Jones, one Wight 840 struck a buoy on the Clyde and had to be repaired. Possibly this was 1401 which was based at Dundee from 15th October 1915 to 23rd March 1916 when it too was struck off charge. Another Wight 840 had three repairs carried out on it before it was sent for service. This was 9021. This aeroplane served at Gibraltar from 1st April to 26th April 1916, when it foundered in rough weather. Another modification that Dalmuir had to carry out for the Wight 840 was to supply and convert a number to dual control with modified controls and windscreens. No other details are known about these aircraft, except that they were trainers.

When order 532 was completed in 1916 it made a loss for the firm of £4879: 5s: 4d, while order 539, due to end in 1916, was continued into 1918 as a batch of thirty Sopwiths and Wight Seaplanes.

The Wight 840 was the least spectacular of all the aeroplanes manufactured at Dalmuir. There was a fundamental weakness with the design and it was not as popular as the Short and latterly, the Fairey Seaplane.

Specification

Type: Torpedo carrying twin float seaplane
Engine: 225 H.P. Sunbeam
Speed: 81M.P.H.
Dimensions: Length 41' 0", Span 61' 0" **Weight**: 4453 lbs.

Wight seaplanes on the River Clyde

Beardmore Wight 840 at Dundee

Nieuport XII

The Nieuport XII evolved from a racing biplane, designed by the Frenchman Gustav Delage for the 1914 Gordon Bennett Cup. From that design there appeared in late 1914 the Nieuport X, its sesquiplane layout becoming a familiar trademark for French Nieuports both of the single - seat variety and as a two-seat reconnaissance biplane. The Nieuport XII appeared in 1915 and was a much stronger and larger aircraft, with a better view for the crew of two and a wider field of fire for the gunner. The pilot sat at the front under the wing, while behind him was the air gunner. The fuselage and tail were of wooden construction covered with fabric. The upper wing consisted of a two spar wooden structure with wire bracing and fabric covering, the lower wing being similar, but with a single spar. The undercarriage was of wood, wire bracing and a rubber chord sprung axle. There were at least two specified power plants for this design, the 110 H.P. and 130 H.P. Clerget, rotary engine and the maximum speed at 6500' was 91 M.P.H.

On the outbreak of the war, the two flying services found themselves heavily dependent on French aero - engines and airframes since both gave speed and performance, which British aircraft lacked. The Admiralty sent a representative to France in the autumn of 1914 to procure aero products and to order aeroplanes. Unfortunately for the Admiralty, the French government took over all contracts for aeroplanes for its own use and contractors were unable to meet their British obligations. It was then arranged, in December 1914, to cancel all these initial contracts since the French government had been asked to supply all the materials required at three monthly intervals, an arrangement that was to be modified from time to time. To avoid competition between the two air services a joint purchasing commission was set up in France in January 1916. Under an earlier arrangement, the Admiralty placed a contract with Beardmore to supply them with fifty Nieuport XIIs during 1915. This contract was allocated the Beardmore number 552 and was to continue for three years. The custom in those times, if no drawings were available, was to send the sub - contractor a sample of the aeroplane that was to be built. In this case the pattern aeroplane was a Nieuport XII designated at Dalmuir as the "Nieuport Experimental Biplane No. 775" and was given the Admiralty Job Number 1095.

In 1916 the order for fifty Nieuports was increased to seventy with an additional order from the R.F.C. for twenty aeroplanes to contract 87A1162, making 552 a joint order for the Admiralty and War Office. A.D.Jones flew the first Nieuport XII, on 10th May 1916 at Dalmuir airfield and the first aeroplanes to be delivered to the R.F.C. commenced during September. The fifty Admiralty Nieuports were in the serial range 9201 to 9250. Twenty of this batch was transferred to the R.F.C., becoming A3270 to A3275 and A3281 to A3294. These Nieuports were used to form 46 squadron at Wyton for corps reconnaissance duties in France. The final batch of Nieuport XIIs which were for the War Office, were serialled A5183 to A5202 and were to be used as operational trainers. Transfer of the Nieuport two seaters between the two services was not unique. Up to January 1917, the Admiralty had transferred 308 aeroplanes to the War Office. Of this total, 100 were Curtis training aeroplanes. Earlier the War Office had transferred 63 aeroplanes, 3 seaplanes and 158 engines to the Admiralty, while the Admiralty transferred 61 engines to the War Office.

The first Nieuport XIIs completed at Dalmuir had horseshoe shaped engine cowlings, a transparent wing panel in the upper wing centre section and a single Lewis machine gun. Later production examples had a fully circular engine cowling, a small fin extension ahead of the rudder, and the transparent centre section covered with fabric, the last aeroplanes of this type being delivered during March 1917. For operations in the Aegean the two - seat Nieuports were modified to have a single Lewis machine gun fixed at an angle through the upper wing centre section and then flown as a single seater. The R.F.C. Nieuports had a single Lewis gun for the observer, fitted to a Scarf ring and a single Vickers firing through the propeller, some others just had a single Lewis gun fitted over the top wing.

Beardmore Nieuports operated with No 1 Wing at San Po, Dunkirk and some of these had the upper wing Lewis gun installation fitted. 9204 served at Dunkirk during 1916 and when it arrived there it was not well received. On the 25th June a report was submitted which was highly critical of the aeroplane's finish and construction. The major criticism was directed at the aircraft's rigging and truing up and it was pointed out that the Beardmore Nieuport XII was inferior to the French built type. When the aeroplane had been flown and dived a loud crack had been heard. The aircraft was inspected and it was found that the damage had been caused by the way it had been manufactured. Here was a problem for the air services that was to continually recur. The Nieuport had been cleared at Dalmuir and accepted for service and the aeroplane had then been delivered and reassembled for flight. The assembly duties were carried out by the R.F.C. However, for the air services themselves, the real problem was finding skilled labour at the factories and the trained personnel at the aircraft-holding units to do the construction work and final assembly accurately.

At Dalmuir, the whole Nieuport batch received modifications and two aeroplanes, 9210 and 9213, were repaired before delivery. Other reports were critical of the aircraft's windscreen size, which was later modified with a smaller type. The R.F.C. Nieuports were also criticised on performance, view and severe engine vibration, which was also a source of criticism from the R.N.A.S. The incorrect fitting of the engine bearers probably caused the vibration to the fuselage longerons. These assembly faults were almost certainly due to lack of drawings, lack of materials and trained aircraft assemblers.

The design of the Nieuport had a unique type of aileron control, resulting in a very complicated system of operation that was very difficult to manufacture or service in the field. When there was a shortage of Sopwith Strutters in April 1917, the Nieuport XII was issued to 45 Squadron. In 1916, the Nieuport could clearly hold its own against the German Air Service, but by 1917 it was clearly obsolete and they were returned from 45 Squadron on 28th May 1917. One of the final batch of two seat Nieuports for the War Office, A5139, was flown by James McCudden V. C. on 8th May 1917 at Wyton, where it was serving with 65 Reserve Squadron.

At Dalmuir the Nieuport Experimental Biplane No 775 survived into 1917 and, for the two years it was at Dalmuir, the work on it had cost the Beardmore Company £1370: 7s: 8d, which they charged to the Admiralty. Then it was given the serial A8967, for write off action by the C. A. D. in 1917, as an engine - less hulk. It certainly was still in existence in February 1918 when it was photographed in the aircraft shed behind a Beardmore Folding Pup. The Ministry of Munitions have on record one Nieuport Two Seater being delivered from Dalmuir, long after production had been completed. Possibly this was A8967.

Specification

Type: Two seat fighter or reconnaissance biplane
Engine: 110 H.P. or 130 H.P. Clerget Rotary
Speed: 96 m. p. h at ground level
Dimensions: Length 23' 11", Height 8' 0 ", Span 29' 7" [upper}, 26' 0" [lower]

9235 at Dalmuir ready for delivery

Single seat Nieuport 12

"N9233" with a training unit

"A/3270" with the R.F.C.

French Nieuport XII   Crashed Nieuport XII

Sopwith Pup

In the spring of 1916, the latest Sopwith design emerged from the company drawing office, called the Sopwith Scout, but to the pilots of the R.N.A.S. and the R.F.C. it became the Sopwith Pup. The Pup was the product of the Sopwith Company's design team that included Herbert Smith, who had joined the company in 1914 from Bristol and Colonial Aircraft. He joined R. J. Ashfield the Project Engineer and his small staff and together they worked on other selected designs. Overseeing the interest of the Sopwith Company was Fred Sigrist who was the company chief engineer. Some of the Sopwith aeroplanes they designed were the Folder, Tabloid and the Gordon Bennett Racer; they also produced a two-seat design called the Sopwith D and a little single - seat biplane for Harry Hawker sometimes called the Sparrow. The Pup stands between the Sopwith Strutter and the Sopwith Triplane in the Sopwith design line and of course from the other aeroplanes mentioned earlier. Many of the Pup's features were common to all the Sopwith designs such as tail, engine cowling, and undercarriage and fuselage structure.

When shown to the military it displayed a common ancestry with the Strutter and Harry Hawker's light biplane and someone at the display said the Strutter had, "Pupped". And so it became the Sopwith Pup. As a biplane, the Pup was very light, powered by the French designed 80 H.P. Clerget rotary engine. Apart from the Royal Aircraft Factory designs, mass production was unheard of in the private aircraft sector. Working drawings were almost unknown; sketches, verbal discussion, chalk marks on the floor for design work, was very much the production rule. The fuselage of the Pup was constructed of wooden longerons and cross members braced with high tensile steel wire and covered with fabric. Towards the nose of the fuselage was a steel torque plate that held the engine. The wings were wire braced, built up from spruce main - spars and lattice ribs covered with fabric. The undercarriage was of the Sopwith pattern, consisting of a tubular Vee with a fabric-covered spreader bar joining the wheels, the shock absorbers being rubber cord with wire bracing. The wing area of the Sopwith Pup was 254 square feet and, as a fighter, carried a single pilot.

    Sopwith were Admiralty contractors, with all six prototypes going to the R.N.A.S. The first prototype Pup, 3691, was built in February 1916 then delivered to Furnes (Belgium) for military trials in May1916. It was an immediate success. There were five other prototypes in the first batch and they were in the serial group 9496 to 9500. Due to the success of the design, the Admiralty placed substantial contracts with Sopwith and their other major naval contractor, William Beardmore & Co, Ltd. With Beardmore, their contract was to be the second batch for fifty aircraft and was in the serial range 9901 to 9950, being allocated the Beardmore number 562, to contract C.P. 117318/16 (or C. P. 113934. Records are not consistently clear about this) and the order was reported to the Beardmore board of directors on 14th July 1916. Following Admiralty practice, the Pup was allocated the serial number 9901. This was the first production Pup built and was flown by A.D.Jones on 26th September 1916 at Dalmuir airfield. The third prototype Pup, 9497 was flown at Dalmuir on the fifth and 13th October 1916 and was probably there to compare the production Beardmore Pups with the Sopwith built variants. The Admiralty accepted 9901 on 16th October 1916. The second Beardmore Pup flew on 23rd October 1916 [9902], the third on 19th November [9903] and so on till 4th May 1917, when the last was delivered for service. Spares for this batch of fifty Pups were covered by the works number 1176 at a cost of £775: 10s: 2d. These spares were also carried into 1917 and 1918.

    During February 1917, the Grand Fleet Aircraft Committee decided to replace the Sopwith Baby floatplane with the Sopwith Pup. The proximity of Dalmuir to Rosyth, the base of the Grand Fleet, meant that Dalmuir received an order to build thirty more Pups, specifically for shipboard use. This batch received the Beardmore number 576, which was in the serial range N6430 to N6459 and they were built to Admiralty contract number AS14757 (or C. P. 105317. Again surviving records not clear). By 1917 order 562 had cost £35612 while 576 worked out at £21000. The Pups of order 576 were different from the initial batch of fifty Pups in order 562, which were type 9901. They were called Type 9901a and were delivered from Dalmuir with a skid undercarriage, an upper wing centre section cut out for an Admiralty fitting for a Lewis gun, (to job number 1202) and provision for flotation air bags in the fuselage and under the lower wing. Although they were all delivered with the skid undercarriage many examples were fitted with the normal wheeled units. Of this second batch of Beardmore Pups, N6430 was flown on the 24th April 1917, N6431 on 1st May 1917, with N6459 being flown on 29th June 1917. An additional form of armament came in the shape of Le Prieur anti-airship rocket apparatus. The rockets were fitted to the aircraft wing struts and resulted in a slight modification to the lower upper wing with metal plates fitted at the strut anchor points. These plates were to protect the aircraft fabric from damage when the rockets fired. The rocket apparatus was manufactured to job number 1174, but later the rockets were replaced with incendiary gun ammunition for the Lewis or Vickers machine guns.

   The Beardmore Pup had three combinations of armament for Admiralty service; Lewis gun with eight rockets, Lewis gun on its own, or eight rockets only. As the war progressed, a Vickers gun was fitted with an interrupter gear, which was either the Sopwith Kauper mechanical gear or the superior Constantinescu gear. The latter worked from the engine through a system of pipes that carried oil at a pulse to the machine gun and stopped the bullets from striking the propeller as it turned.

   The Grand Fleet Aircraft Committee in February 1917 had recommended that the light cruiser class all be fitted with aeroplanes, including the hybrid carrier H.M.S. Campania for anti – airship work. The light cruisers included H.M.S. Yarmouth, H.M.S. Caledon and H.M.S. Cordelia. Two of the great advocates of using landplanes at sea were A. M. Longmore and Flight Commander F. J. Rutland, who had both approached the Grand Fleet Aircraft Committee and insisted that the Beardmore Pups be allocated to all capital ships. The Admiralty regarded the Zeppelin as its greatest menace and needed proof that landplanes could be a success at sea. On 29th April 1917, Rutland flew off the deck of H.M.S. Manxman in an area known to be frequented by Zeppelins. His Beardmore Pup had been modified by strapping an air bag as a flotation unit to the outside of the fuselage. Rutland found no Zeppelin and unfortunately for him when he landed in the sea the bag kept the Pup afloat for only about twenty minutes before sinking. Later the first Beardmore Pup 9901 was utilised for ditching trials at the Isle of Grain. When fitted with Beardmore manufactured air bags it floated for six hours. Then came a success, a success that fully vindicated the use of aeroplanes at sea.

In June came the first flight of a Beardmore Pup flown by F. J. Rutland from the deck of the light cruiser. H.M.S. Yarmouth had been converted at Rosyth to carry an aeroplane and a twenty-foot platform was built on her deck above the forward gun. On 21st August 1917, on his first take off from Yarmouth in a Beardmore Pup, Flight Sub - Lieutenant B.A. Smart shot down the Zeppelin L23. The Minister of Munitions, Winston Churchill, was most impressed by this victory. What impressed him more was the cost of the Pup, which was "... only the discharge of a heavy gun in value." When the Pup ditched beside H.M.S. Prince it was lost, but the pilot was saved. For the Germans all they found of their airship were pieces of burnt fabric and a charred propeller.

The conversion programme for the Light Cruiser force had been carried out under the direction of Rear Admiral Phillimore, but Wing Captain R. M. Groves carried out the Yarmouth conversion. After the success of the destruction of the airship L23, one light cruiser in each light cruiser squadron was fitted with a flying off forward deck and this included H.M.S. Cassandra. The achievement of these flying - off decks using Beardmore Pups led to a fundamental re - think in the use of air power at sea. Floatplane carriers were clearly obsolete. The Royal Navy was now to concentrate on building aircraft carriers and using landplanes at sea. The problem was how to get an aeroplane off the deck and into the air with the minimum of fuss and the maximum of safety.

As early as 26th December 1916 two Beardmore Pups of the first production batch of fifty had been assigned to H.M.S. Vindex. In March 1917 two were sent to the Isle of Grain to carry out dummy deck landing trials. Trials were also undertaken at Hendon to try to develop a launching catapult for aircraft use. For these experiments two Pups were delivered straight from Dalmuir; these were 9948 and 9949. The idea of the catapult had been in discussion since 1914. Drawings exist of an electrical generator for an Admiralty catapult dated 29th May 1914, at the Paisley firm of Fullarton, Hodgart and Barclay. They built a hydraulic catapult for the Admiralty, but their catapult design was shelved until the Hendon trials. Trials were also undertaken on board the converted collier H.M.S. Slinger. On one trial a sheep was used to replace the crew and when the trial commenced the sheep disappeared into the aeroplane to the howls of laughter from the watching dignitaries.

Then the flying - off trials moved forward to another development. Lieutenant Commander G. H. B. Cowan suggested that ramps be built between the gun barrels of capital ships. To help the Pups take off, the turrets could be turned without the ship having to turn into wind. Experiments to prove Cowan's idea were conducted on the battle cruiser H.M.S. Repulse in the Firth of Forth under the direction of Captain J. S. Dumaresq. On 7th October 1917, Squadron Commander Rutland took a chance. "B" turret of Repulse was trained at an angle of 42° to starboard and Rutland flew off successfully in his Pup N6453. Seven days later he repeated his success when he flew off Repulse's 15" after turret. These trials proved that aeroplanes could be flown off the turrets of capital ships successfully, without hindering their true operational role. Wheeled aeroplanes could now be carried by most ships and operate in fleet activities with the fitting turret platforms beginning almost at once in the autumn of 1917.

As these battle - cruiser trials were taking place, the Light Battle – Cruiser, H.M.S. Furious was taken in hand by her builders. This ship was a hybrid, built for operations in the Baltic, with a draught of fifteen feet and she had two consorts, H.M.S. Glorious and H.M.S. Courageous. Furious differed from the last two ships in having a huge

18" gun on her after turret. All her heavy gun armament was moved when towards the bow she was modified as an aircraft carrier. This was carried out in two phases; firstly, a platform was built over her forward deck, then secondly the aft 18" gun was removed for landing on deck trials. By July 1917, H.M.S. Furious had joined the Grand Fleet at its northern base, Scapa Flow, in the Orkneys. She was allocated seven Sopwith Pups, which were based at Smoogro and she had two seaplanes for reconnaissance duties. Five of these seven aeroplanes have been identified as being built at Dalmuir; they were N6438, N6452, N6453 (used in the Repulse trials), N6454, and N6455. Under the forward sloping deck of Furious was the aircraft hangar, her forward turret having been removed. The C.O. of the Pup squadron was Squadron Commander Dunning and he was most impressed with his pilots. At the end of each training day, before they would land at Smoogro the pilots would fly along the side of Furious and run their aircraft wheels along the 228' foot deck, controlling their approach by "blipping" the engine. This inspired Dunning.

Without the knowledge of his immediate superior, or informing him of his plans, Dunning attempted to land on the forward deck of H.M.S. Furious. On 2nd August 1917, Dunning, flying a Beardmore Pup, landed on the fore - deck of H.M.S. Furious. As his aircraft came in it drifted over the centre of the deck, rope toggles hanging from the Pup were grabbed by the deck crew and as Dunning cut the engine the Pup was landed (pulled would be better) to the deck. This was the very first time an aeroplane had been landed on a moving ship at sea. Still without informing the Admiralty or his superiors, E. H. Dunning tempted the fates again five days later and this time they were not so forgiving. His first attempt was a success, but the wind was gusting and in catching the aircraft, an elevator was damaged. By his third attempt he had changed to Pup N6452. As he came into land, he was too far forward. He waved the deck party away and then opened the throttle fully, but the engine lost power. The Pup stalled, came down heavily on its starboard wheel and fell over the side of the ship. The Pup then landed in front of the moving carrier with H.M.S. Furious sailing over the stranded flyer. The Pup was fitted with air bags and when it was recovered, it was found that Dunning had been knocked unconscious in the cockpit and had drowned.

A Sopwith Sparrow

The Sopwith Churchill

9914 at East Fortune 1917

Pup/WBIII on ditching trials

H.M.S. Furious with 18" gun

Rope barrier on H.M.S. Furious

The stern of H.M.S. Vindictive

7th August 1917, Dunning's first landing

Recovering Dunning in N6452

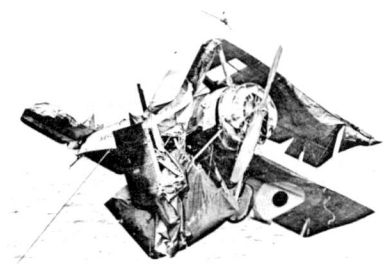
Wreckage hoisted aboard Furious

N6452 on the deck of Furious

N6453 27th August 1917

"Excuse Me" at the Isle of Grain

Into the rope barrier Furious 1918

Low approach to stern

Possibly N6453 with H.M.S. Furious

N6453 on B turret H.M.S. Repulse

N6443 on the battlecruiser H.M.S Tiger

W.B.III N6100 on H.M.S. Cassandra

W.B.III and N6708 under test at the Isle of Grain

On 27th August 1917, Squadron Commander Busteed flew N6453 off Furious, but by then the trials were abandoned by order of the Admiralty. However, in October 1917 Sub Lt. W. D. Jackson flew from Donibristle to Furious for still more trials. He made five runs at Furious while she was steaming into wind. He found that there was severe turbulence around the Pup, there were no deck markings, a poor view from the cockpit and a lack of a properly calibrated rev-counter to help him make a safe deck landing. It was then decided that Furious be taken out of service and be fitted with a landing on platform on her after deck. She re-joined the fleet in March 1918, but she still had the clumsy funnel and bridge superstructure in the middle of her hull. Furious was not flush decked. For her arrester trials she carried the fore and aft wire system designed by G. H. E. Whiteway, Assistant Constructor, Naval Construction Department of the Admiralty. Two 9901a Pups carried out these tests on 15th April 1918 and they proved Jackson's tests correct. On the test flights one pilot could not position the Pup correctly, one bumped into the buffer net behind the funnel and Squadron Commander Rutland's Pup struck the lift - well and fell upside down over the port side and onto the torpedo tubes.

The majority of the Dalmuir built Pups saw service at sea with the R.N.A.S. N6443, which was first flown at Dalmuir on 30th May 1917, saw service aboard H.M.S. Manxman after delivery to Turnhouse near Edinburgh. It then saw service aboard the magnificent Clyde - built battlecruiser H.M.S. Tiger of Jutland fame. The converted cross - channel packet H.M.S. Manxman carried 9913, 9943, 9945, N6431, N6444 and N6445. H.M.S. Vindex was allocated 9921, N6457 and N6458. For land use, three Beardmore Pups were at Imbros in the Mediterranean. These were 9942, N6432 and N6433, one having the Lewis gun on the top wing and the Vickers gun ahead of the pilot, 9942 surviving the Armistice. At Imbros, their performance was utilised to the fullest as airship protection for the patrolling anti-submarine airship scouts. When one anti-submarine airship was on patrol, a single Pup would accompany it and loiter at altitude, out of harm's way.

By the end of 1917 and the beginning of 1918, the Pup was clearly obsolete even for shipboard use with the R.N.A.S., but a new use for the Pup was found by March 1918 and that was training. The training programme built around the D. H. 6 had been dropped and it was entirely reconstructed around the Avro 504. Due to production difficulties the whole programme had to operate on a mix of the D. H. 6 and Sopwith Pups. This meant that production of the Sopwith Pup was continued well into the autumn of 1918. In all, over 1800 Sopwith Pups were built for the Admiralty, War Office and finally the Royal Air Force.

By 1918 the order for Wight seaplanes had been completed, but the Beardmore number 539 for the Wight seaplanes was resurrected again. This became a joint order of Wight Seaplanes and thirty Sopwith Pups. They were manufactured for the Admiralty at Dalmuir with the Ministry of Munitions acting as supply agent, but there are no serials existing for this batch. What is definitely known is that Dalmuir manufactured eighty Sopwith Pups and that one was taken from the production line and converted. The Admiralty felt that a variant of the Sopwith Pup should be built to replace the Sopwith Baby seaplanes on H.M.S. Campania. One Beardmore Pup, 9950, was taken from the production line and modified. The aircraft that emerged from the Beardmore modification programme had all wing stagger eliminated with the wings being able to fold. In 1913 T. O. M. Sopwith had taken out a wing-folding patent and the design of this was incorporated into the modified Sopwith Pup. The fuselage was built twelve inches longer than the standard Pup by fitting an extra bay behind the engine mount and the wings being shortened by eighteen inches so that when they folded they would not foul the external flying surfaces of the tail. Another interesting feature that 9950 had was the ability of the undercarriage to fold up for storage on a ship. Beardmore had completed the modifications to the Pup to Aviation Contract (Admiralty), numbers 1185 and 1187, up to 31st December 1916. With this change in appearance, the Sopwith Pup got a change of name when it was called, "Aeroplane Folding Scout S. B.3d Type" with the Beardmore order Number 579 for one hundred aeroplanes. Spares for the Folding Scouts were manufactured to Admiralty job number 1292. The first production example N6100 was repaired at Dalmuir and it had the folding undercarriage, as did the rest up to N6112. The first prototype was not flown at Dalmuir. With a change in

Ministry of Munitions' policy, it was crated and taken by rail to Eastchurch, for test. There Harry Busteed flew it on 17th February 1917. The first production S. B.3d was flown by A.D.Jones at Dalmuir on 25th June 1917, the second on 6th July 1917 and so on to October, when N6127 flew on the twenty - third of that month. N61298 and N6129 were at Donibristle and Rosyth during the winter of 1917.There were thirty engineless airframes, N6702 to N6731, with the exception of N6708, which was flown and tested at the Isle of Grain in January 1918. One of the requirements for the Folding Pup was that it should be able to float once it landed in the water and so air bags were installed in its fuselage. These air bags, designed by Harry Busteed and called "Busteed Gear," came in different marks; Mk. IVs were installed in the fuselage with the Mk.I being fitted onto the lower wing. The Mk. IV came in five types, "a" to "e" with the Mk. IVb being fitted to the first bay in the S. B.3d (and the Pup), Mk. IVc to the second bay, IVd to the third bay and IVe to the fourth bay. Both bags were inflated by an air bottle from inside the cockpit. The whole S.B.3d production programme was carried out to Munitions contract number A. S.775.

All one hundred were delivered through 1917 to 1918 and cost £63485: 4s: 2d to produce. The design was a joint venture of Sopwith and Beardmore, with G. T. Richards being in charge of the programme. This joint order is reflected in the name S. B.3d, S for Sopwith, B for Beardmore. All through the surviving Beardmore and Ministry of Munitions documents the aeroplane is called "Folding Scout S. B.3d", giving credence to G.T. Richards's belief that it was not a true Beardmore design, but a modification of an existing type. Many of its features were not a success, such as the folding undercarriage and folding wings. N6101 was fitted with a dropping undercarriage, weighing twenty - one pounds and from N6113 all the S. B.3ds were fitted with this device.

When Lieutenant Moore was testing this aircraft, at the Isle of Grain, he was able to drop his undercarriage and land successfully in the water. The redesigned Pup with its drastic modifications was not an improvement on the original design. It reportedly had an improvement in endurance, which was a major Admiralty requirement, but its single Lewis machine gun was clearly inadequate.

The S.B.3d did not see any warlike action, though many were assigned to units of the Grand Fleet. N6115 went to the battle cruiser H.M.S. Renown for fly off trials, H.M.S. Nairana carried three, N6105, N6108 and N6110 and another three went to H.M.S. Pegasus .(N6104, N6106 and N6107) Of the one hundred S. B.3s ordered from Beardmore only thirty six were flown at Dalmuir. The balance were crated and delivered to the R.N.A.S. by rail. On 30th November 1918 the Royal Air Force had on charge a total of 52 S. B.3ds with three being written off in November, eighteen were stored at Renfrew Acceptance Park and thirty four were with the Grand Fleet. Others are reported as being sent to Japan with a British mission, while many were broken up as spares, the type being declared obsolete during February 1918.

In 1921, when Dalmuir was clearing out the remnants of its Aviation Department, £1615 was made on the sale of scrap materials belonging to order 576, once a batch of thirty Beardmore manufactured Sopwith Pups.

(i)

Specification

Type: Single seat scout
Engine: 80 H.P. Le Rhone, 80 H.P. Gnome, 80 H.P. Clerget.
Dimensions: Span: 26' 6" Length: 19' 3", Height: 9' 5"

(ii)

Pups on order
1 March 1917 815
1 March 1918 394

(iii)

**Delivery of aeroplanes for ship's use,
Sopwith Folder S.B. 3d**

1917	June	July	August	Sept	Oct	Nov	Dec	1918	Jan	Feb	Mar
	1	4	7	2	17	26	26		14	3	0

(iv)

Delivery of aeroplanes Sopwith Scout
1st January 1917 to 1st March 1918

Jan	Feb	Mar	Apr	May	Jun	Jul	Aug	Sept	Oct	Nov	Dec	Jan	Feb	Mar
25	41	71	80	97	80	65	50	95	93	119	132	166	173	161

(v)

R.A.F. Sopwith Pups on charge 30th November 1918

332	in store	13	Grand Fleet /Northern Patrol
2	at Acceptance Parks	1	14 Wing Italy
58	S. E. Area	2	In transit
42	S. W. Area	5	Mediterranean
64	Midland Area	48	Egypt and Palestine
41	N.E. Area	42	Written off in November
31	N. W. Area	93	Schools
13	Sundry Duties	21	C. T. D.

(vi)

Total requirement for Seaplanes and Aeroplane for Ship's use

	1 Jan/30 June 1918	1 July/31 Dec 1918	1 Jan/ 30 June 1919
Sopwith Scout S. B.3d 2F.1	208	252	324

(vii)

Requirement for training machines R.F.C. 10. 10. 17 Sopwith Scout
(Includes 237 for additional machines, which can be Camels)

1917			1918							
Oct	Nov	Dec	Jan	Feb	Mar	Apr	May	Jun	Jul	Aug
193	99	99	69	69	69	69	99	137	152	125

(viii)

R.A.F. Sopwith 9901a on Charge
30 November 1918

10 With Grand Fleet

(ix)

H.M.S. Furious [1918]
Builder: Armstrong Whitworth **Launched** 15 August 1916
Dimensions: Length: 786' 6", Beam: 88' **Displacement:** 22000 tons
Geared Turbines: 4 shafts; 94000 S.H.P. **Speed:** 32.5 knots
Planes: 20 **Complement:** 737
Note: Launched with one 18" gun and fore - part as carrier, gun removed to monitors when refitted. Launched first carrier strike 1918, reconstructed, withdrawn Mediterranean Fleet, reconstructed flush-decked 1921 to 1925. Home Fleet; 1939 to 1944: raids on Tirpitz 1944. Reserve 1944 to 1945. Scrapped Dalmuir 15th March 1948 and Troon [hull] 22nd June 1948.

(x)

Test report of Sopwith Scout
Serial A653, built by Standard Motors, dated 9th May 1917 by Controller Technical Department [C. T. D.] Ministry of Munitions
No. of crew: One **Duty:** Fighter **Engine:** 100 H.P. Mono
Speed at 10000': Revs: 1180 = 101.5 M.P.H. **Speed at 15000' Revs:** 1105 = 94.5 M.P.H. **Ceiling approximately** = 20000' **Endurance at full speed** = 1.75 hrs.
Total weight fully loaded = 1297 lbs. **Climb to 6500'** 7 mins 10 secs at Revs. 1045
Climb to 10000' 13 mins 0 secs at Revs. 1030
Military Load = Pilot: 180 lbs. **Vickers Gun:** 35 lbs. **Deadweight:** 45 lbs.

N6454 on Furious

On the deck of Furious

Sopwith 2F-1 Camel

The deployment of the Sopwith 2F-1 Ship's Camel with units of the Grand Fleet in 1917 represented a bold move by the Admiralty, but such a move during a critical phase of the Great War was beset with difficulty. When the Ministry of Munitions took over all aeroplane production in the spring of 1917, there were shortages in skilled labour, raw materials, finance and accurate production figures. Like all ministries, the Ministry of Munitions functioned on statistics, but there were no accurate figures available for the Supply Department to base any forward planning on aircraft production; many of the figures were unreliable and were more of a guess rather than an estimate. Strikes also dominated this period; they were disastrous for the aircraft programme because of the complexity and the nature of the supply of aircraft and the use of sub - contracts. The Air Board also added confusion to the situation by changing its priority with the aircraft manufacturers. They decided that aircraft manufacturers with purpose built factories should get all the contracts to build aeroplanes, while the others would build aeroplanes on a sub - contract basis. This put the Sopwith company in a predicament because they built their aircraft in a converted ice - rink. In July 1917, Sopwiths were told to cease aeroplane manufacture and concentrate on the supply of spare parts. To add more confusion to the issue, the manufacturers had to obtain permission and advice from the Controller of Aeronautical Supplies before placing any sub - contract orders. Then, during September 1917, the Air Board reversed its earlier decision and decided to concentrate manufacturing capacity not with small contractors, but with large purpose - built units, leaving Sopwith and others to produce aeroplanes on their own.

   It was then decided to build three National Aeroplane Factories with a production capacity of two hundred aeroplanes a month and sites were chosen at Croydon, Liverpool, and Richmond. Sopwiths were initially in favour of the scheme, but due to the terms of the financial arrangements opted out. Sopwith then took out the lease on the Richmond premises and the Ministry built a replacement at Heaton Chapel, Manchester. The Sopwith factory was to be built at a cost of £200000 in October 1917, with a projected production target of four hundred aeroplanes a month by the end of June 1918. Ultimately, the whole scheme was a failure and a financial embarrassment and never worked. During this period, Sopwith were producing more examples of the Sopwith "Zoo," such as the Hippo, Dolphin and Camel. The Sopwith Camel first appeared in the autumn of 1916 and it earned its name due to the compactness of the armament above the engine ahead of the cockpit. The first prototype was passed by the Sopwith Experimental Department on 22nd December 1916 and even with shortages and political intrusion, the first Camel was delivered to the R.N.A.S. on 7th May 1917.

During January 1917, Sopwith proceeded with a design for the Sopwith Baby replacement based on the Sopwith Camel. This aircraft was to be called the Sopwith Camel Seaplane F. S. 1 and was to be powered by the 130 H.P., Clerget rotary engine. The Sopwith drawing was D2079, being approved by Herbert Smith and retraced by J. B. McKeowan during 1917. Using Admiralty practice, two prototypes were ordered serialled N4 and N5. The evolution of the F. S. 1 was affected by a series of decisions out-with Sopwith's control including the Admiralty decision to move away from floatplane fighters.

There is uncertainty as to whether N4 was built or not. There are reports that it flew in March 1917 and crashed that same month, but the N4 story has a Beardmore twist. William Beardmore at his victory dinner speech declared that Dalmuir had built Sopwith Baby Seaplanes. When N4 crashed it was referred to as an "improved Baby". Now, Dalmuir had an Admiralty Job Number for work on a Baby Seaplane. In 1916 repairs were carried out on a Sopwith Baby to job no. 1118. This number re - appears in 1917 as, "Attendance at trial flights for Baby Sopwith" and again in 1918, but this time with the addition, "...... with yacht tenders." Certainly, there is no doubt that N5 was built and has often been reported as a wheeled version of the Sopwith Camel Seaplane, since many of the design features were the same: armament, engine, split fuselage for ship storage and the run of the control lines. During 1917, it was found that the twin Vickers installation built into the Sopwith Camel was a source of servicing difficulty. Kauper of Sopwith was asked to demonstrate dismantling, stripping and re - installation of the weapons, since it was he who had designed the layout and the interrupter gear. It took him four hours to remove one gun and it was clear that the twin Vickers installation would be unworkable at sea. The preferred armament of the 2F-1 then became one Vickers gun and one overwing Lewis gun.

Another factor for ordering the 2F-1 was overproduction of the Sopwith Pup and the S.B.3d. At the time, early 1917, both of these types had been ordered in excess of requirement. When aeroplanes and seaplanes were ordered, the Ministry of Munitions recommended that four and a half months' notice be given to the contractors for continuation of an existing type and six months' notice for contracts on new types. The Ship's Camel came within the period of the Ministry's recommendations and so a delay for ordering the type occurred.

Fifty production 2F-1s were ordered from the Sopwith Company in September 1917 for delivery in October that year and they were in the serial range N6600 to N6649. All were delivered in the specified time. These 2F-1s were powered by the penultimate British rotary engine the Admiralty Rotary 1 (A.R.1) which was designed by W.O. Bentley of motor car fame. Later this engine became the B.R. 1. The Ship's Camel had its fuselage split for ease of erection and for recovery or storage, and the control lines were made external so that they would not foul the internal air bags of the flotation gear. By the late autumn of 1917, it was clear that Sopwith could not handle a follow on order for the 2F-1; the Ministry of Munitions therefore placed an order with Beardmore at Dalmuir. The contract was placed on 22nd November 1917 and initially the contract, A.S.35920, was for fifty aircraft in the serial range N6750 to N6799. Later another batch of fifty was ordered, N6800 to N6849, to contract A. S.2301/18, making one hundred Sopwith 2F-1 Ship's Camels to be built at Dalmuir. Beardmore allocated the order 598 to these aeroplanes and by the end of the year the Admiralty had concluded that the most suitable fighter to take to sea was the Camel.

The 2F-1 was constructed along similar lines to the Sopwith Pup; the wings were built up around wooden main spars and ribs, which were braced with wire, the whole structure being covered with fabric. The fuselage and tail were built in a similar fashion to the Pup's, with a tubular, rubber-sprung undercarriage.

A prototype 2F-1 on the workshop bench, possibly at Dalmuir as a pattern 1918

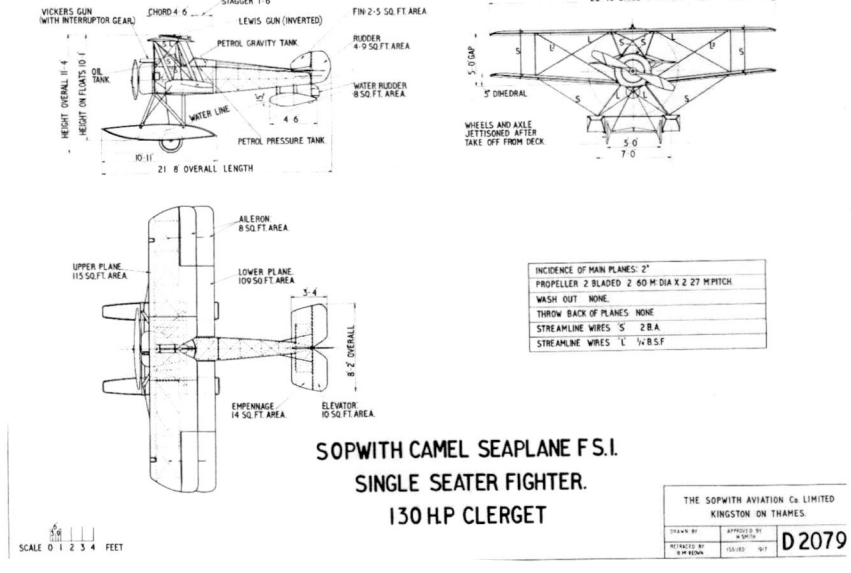

The drawing of the Sopwith Camel Seaplane F.S.1

Prototype 2F-1 Camel N5 with rockets   Two Camels at Turnhouse, Edinburgh

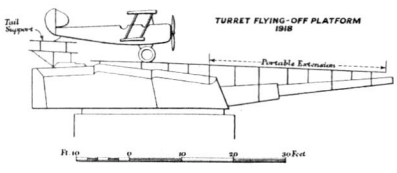 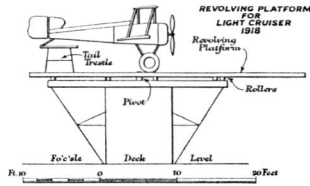

Gun turret and revolving ramps for capital ships

A 2F-1 leaves H.M.S. Barham   Fully armed 2F-1 leaves Melbourne

Leaving the carrier vessel Pegasus   The cruiser H.M.S. Galatea

All 2F-1s were powered by the 150 H.P. A. R. 1 (B.R. 1), but the alternative powerplant was the 130 H.P. Clerget. Comparative trials for these two aero - engines was carried out on 24th May 1917 (Clerget) and 22nd May 1917 (A. R. 1) and proved the superiority of the A. R. 1. The Bentley engine was also specified for other Camels built by Nieuport (AS 14412/AS 17565) and those of Clayton and Shuttleworth (AS.7861/AS.23979). Some of these Camels were used by the Admiralty for ditching trials or tested with the dropping undercarriage.

By March 1918 the Beardmore order 598 was increased by the addition of another batch of fifty Camels bringing the order to 150. During early February 1918 a Sopwith 2F-1 Camel, N6618, was at Dalmuir and by 2nd March 1918, four Beardmore Camels had been manufactured. Beardmore Camels had detailed changes, particularly in relation to the prototype N5: the engine panels were a different shape, there was a chute for spent cartridge cases and linkages, the elevator cables were fitted externally, the windscreen was a different shape, there was a Lewis gun on an Admiralty mount and a wind driven generator on the starboard cabane strut. Dalmuir also received another order for thirty 2F-1s, to which the number 609 was given. The other order, 598, was costed at £145131: 15s: 8d. N6750 was the first Beardmore Camel and it flew at Dalmuir on 20th February 1918. It was delivered to Rosyth for ship duty, together with N6751 to N6754.

Turnhouse, near Edinburgh, received N6755 to N6773 and the last of the first hundred Camels, N6849, was at Renfrew Acceptance Park in August 1918. As well as Camel spares, some modifications were carried out by Beardmore for the Admiralty. The 2F-1 had problems with its fuel system and fifty-four sets of petrol piping were supplied to the Admiralty. Thirty sets of main spar box sockets were also provided. Two special Camel centre sections together with slings were specially made and eighty release hooks for use on ramps and lighters. Production at Dalmuir would seem to be ahead of all expectation, with twenty expected to be delivered in April 1918. In fact thirty were delivered. The Beardmore production target for the 2F-1 was eleven per week. All the Camels were first flown at Dalmuir, taken to Renfrew Aircraft Acceptance Park for stability and rigging tests by the

Aeronautical Inspection Department, who then handed the aeroplanes over to the Acceptance Branch of the R.N.A.S./R.A.F. It was at Renfrew that any faults were rectified with the aircraft. For the supply of aeroplanes the Ministry of Munitions wanted the first ten to be assembled at the factory with the balance being crated and sent to the acceptance parks, with one in ten of the remainder being assembled and flown at the contractors. The proximity of Renfrew and the location of Dalmuir to the Grand Fleet meant that these conditions could be waived.

The armament of the Ship's Camel was its most interesting feature: a single Vickers machine gun fitted to the port side of the fuselage and a drum fed Lewis machine gun. Dalmuir retained one Camel, N7132 for gun trials. The standard interrupter gear was the Constantinescu Gear type C. The type B had been developed in May 1917 and was replaced by the later type of gear. Over the top wing it had a Lewis machine gun on an Admiralty Mount that could be pulled down for reloading. When the Camel arrived with units of the R.N.A.S. it quickly replaced the Sopwith/Beardmore Pup aboard vessels of the Grand Fleet.

On 1st June 1918, the Beardmore Ship's Camel was at sea and in action. Harwich Force was at sea and in their locality was a flotilla of German minesweepers that had been warned by seaplanes that the Royal Navy was in the area. Spotting the seaplanes, the Camels from Melbourne and Sydney took off. The Camel from Sydney shot down one seaplane, but due to gun trouble could not follow up its success. On 18th June 1918, gun trouble once again caused an inconclusive action. The first Light Cruiser Squadron was at sea with H.M.S. Furious when two seaplanes attacked them. Two of her Camels flew off, N6801 and N6810, but could not press home their attacks due to gun stoppages. When they returned to Furious, they landed in the sea beside a destroyer and were recovered. That same day the Camel from H.M.S. Galatea was lost when it intercepted another seaplane, but was interned in Denmark after the action. During this period Galatea is known to have had two Beardmore Camels allocated, N7116 and N7126. Obviously, from these actions, the main adversary for the Camels was the German seaplane, but the Admiralty still regarded the Zeppelin as the real threat to its operations. Earlier, on 20th May 1918,

Camels had flown off the Light Cruisers H.M.S. Phaeton and H.M.S. Royalist to intercept a patrolling airship, but due to bad visibility, no combat took place. The Royal Navy now felt that if the Zeppelins would not come to the navy, the navy would go to the Zeppelins. The German airships were based at Tondern north of Sylt, which had double airship sheds and the Admiralty prepared a plan.

Two attack flights were formed using 2F-1 Camels from H.M.S. Furious. Originally, their base was Turnhouse and they were able to train at East Fortune because the airship sheds there were similar to the German ones. At the end of June the two flights were embarked upon Furious at Rosyth and she left for her mission on 27th June. As she crossed the North Sea with the cruisers from the First Light Cruiser Squadron she met bad weather and had to return. The second attempt took place on 17th July, but she was again delayed a day due to a heavy thunderstorm. When she arrived at her designated station on 19th July, H.M.S. Furious flew off two flights of seven Ship's Camels (five were built at Dalmuir) for the attack on the airship sheds. The first flight had three Camels flown by Captain W. F. Dickinson, Captain W. D. Jackson and Lieutenant N.E. Williams. The second flight was of four Camels flown by Captain B.A. Smart of Yarmouth fame, Captain Thyne and Lieutenants Dawson and Yeullett. The first building to be attacked was the ammunition shed. The Camels then attacked one of the airship sheds, but flew off quickly to conserve fuel. Captain Dickinson landed beside a destroyer and was saved, but the other two flew off towards Denmark. There Captain Jackson destroyed his Camel while the other was interned. Before the next attack by the second flight one aeroplane was lost when it ditched due to engine trouble. This was Captain Thyne's Camel. The other three pressed home the attack on the other airship shed, then flew back to the carrier; Captain Smart alighted beside the destroyer H.M.S. Violent, Lieutenant Yeullett ditched in the sea, but unfortunately was drowned while Lieutenant Dawson flew off to Denmark and was interned. Possibly his aeroplane was N6823. As a result of the Tondern raid, two airships were destroyed, L54 and L60, while one of the airship sheds was severely damaged. This raid was an unquestionable success and fulfilled all the military demands of the

Admiralty, proving conclusively the worth of having aeroplanes at sea.

The earlier success of flying off Sopwith Pups from gun turrets with ramps led to another development. It was suggested to Lord Weir, now Air Minister, that ramps be fitted to flying boat lighters. The earliest suggestion to Lord Weir came on 1st March 1918 when he was still, only just, with the Ministry of Munitions. This suggestion came from the Deputy Controller Technical Department in his notes on marine aircraft policy, but as early as September 1916 the idea had been suggested by Squadron Commander Porte. The official history, "The War in the Air," gives the credit to Admiral Tyrwhitt and Commander C. R. Samson who took up the idea. The plan was that a flying boat lighter be planked over, an aeroplane installed on the new deck and the whole vessel be towed by a destroyer at 30 knots and by using a special release clip on the undercarriage an aircraft would take off. Messrs' Thorneycroft carried out the whole modification programme and the first trial took place at Felixstowe on 30th May 1918.

Samson had taken a standard Sopwith built 2F-1 Camel, N6623 and had it fitted with a skid undercarriage similar to the 9901a Pup. When the trial started things did not go at all well. Two troughs had been fitted to the platform to engage the skids and experience had shown that the tail would be damaged if it was not supported in some way. For this trial Major Cadbury lay on his back and supported the tail. When Samson tried to get the Camel into the air one skid was caught in a trough, the aeroplane cart wheeled over the bow and Commander Samson was lucky to survive the ducking. The towing destroyer H.M.S. Truculent, which had altered course to avoid a sandbar, had caused the accident. With the change in course, the lighter made a slight angle causing the Camel to jump the trough. The skid undercarriage was obviously useless and for the next trial a standard Beardmore built Camel, N6812, was used with wheels. After choosing a new pilot by lot, Lieutenant S. D. Culley took of successfully on the 31st July 1918. To stop the lighter porpoising (this had happened during Samson's first attempt) the crew of the lighter successfully laid themselves down at the bow. Next day N6812 was sent to Martlesham Heath for gun trials.

Commander Samson had made plans to intercept a Zeppelin airship, but after his accident with the skid Camel, he was advised not to undertake any flying. Stuart Culley took his place. In his detailed scheme for the airship intercept Samson had made plans for the armament fit. Since this was a one – off intercept, the Camel could be fitted with ether twin Vickers guns, or one Vickers and one Lewis gun, or twin Lewis guns with incendiary ammunition. In the plans Culley was also given directions on how to attack the airship. He was not to attack from below or behind its tail, but to attack at the airship's blind spot, which was to the front above the nose, with his first pass. By 9th August, N6812 had been fitted with twin Lewis guns on the upper wing the single Vickers having been removed. But the over wing twin Lewis installation meant that a reload in flight was impossible.

On 11th August 1918 Lieutenant S. D. Culley took off from a lighter H3, towed by H.M.S. Redoubt. He could not follow the rules of engagement set out by Samson, simply because the Camel did not have the performance at altitude that he wanted, but he still shot down L53 with his Lewis guns. During November 1918 the London Gazette published Culley's D. S. O. award in less than ten lines, denying the young officer the promised Victoria Cross. Due to the conditions on board the lighter the mechanic who swung the propeller also received a decoration for his bravery and that was the Air Force Medal.

One of the more spectacular trials for the Beardmore 2F-1 Camel was the airship parasite trials at Pulham Norfolk during the summer of 1918. A horizontal airflow surface was fitted to the Vickers airship R23 and a Camel was attached to it. The first trial was carried out with a pilotless Camel with its controls locked and carrying a dummy pilot. When the Camel was dropped it glided to the ground turning over when it landed. Lieutenant Keys had a successful release in the Camel N6814. He was able to start the engine, fly around R23 and then land at Pulham. After the war the trials continued with a variety of methods, but it was left to the Americans to develop the concept of an airship carrying its own fighters for self-defence.

After the war the 2F-1 Camel was used extensively for aircraft carrier trials with major units of the fleet. Even with the Armistice, production of the Camel was still being recorded as continuing at

Dalmuir. The Air Board had decided that Beardmore should cease building the Camel in June 1918 and concentrate production on the V/1500. All the jigs, drawings and materials were to have been passed on to the firm of Pegler, but for some reason Arrol - Johnston built the last ten of the order for 150 Camels. When they were built at Heathfield the Camels were assembled from parts supplied by Dalmuir. This may explain why order 609, reported as cancelled, was continued into 1921 when the type was still in production for the R.A.F. Some of these Camels saw service in Russia during the War of Intervention against the Bolshevik forces.

A 2F-1 on gun ramp aboard Sydney   N6812 aboard the lighter H3 July 1918

On board H.M.S.Furious being prepared for the Tondern raid

N6779 being recovered

Pilot of a 2F-1 on H.M.A.S. Australia

Stuart Culley in centre, possibly with part of the crew of lighter H3

N6812 restored as a 2F-1

N6812 on display in the spring of 1994

Culley with his Camel

A 2F-1 leaves a battleship

Many were left with the emerging countries from the collapsed Russian Empire, such as Latvia, since it was economically impossible to bring them home. Many of the Camels were also incapable of being flown since they were in poor mechanical condition to be returned home and were left behind when the British forces withdrew.

Nine 2F-1 Camels were sent to Canada and served at Camp Borden until 1928, some of the nine having been built by Arrol - Johnston. Today Canada has one of the surviving Sopwith 2F-1 Camels, which was built by Hooper. N8156 served at Camp Borden and was restored to flying condition by C. R. Sawson in 1966 - 67 and was flown in June 1967 by Wing Commander P.A. Hartman. This Camel was the first Bentley powered Camel to take to the air since the 1920s and is now preserved at Rockliffe in Canada.

After the war N6812 was selected for preservation by the Air Ministry and was donated to the Imperial War Museum and stored at Cardington. It was displayed in 1931 in its original condition at the Imperial War Museum. When the museum was refurbished in 1938, N6812 was put on display and proved a popular exhibit. In 1941 it was damaged during the London Blitz and after restoration by a Royal Air Force maintenance unit it was put on display as a Camel F1 with the spurious serial F4043. In 1955 an attempt was made to restore it to its original configuration as a Ship's Camel and bearing its true identity. In 1963 Stuart Culley visited the museum and saw the Camel after it was restored. He disputed the underside colour of N6812 and told the restorers to scratch the paint from the struts. When this was done the blue paint was revealed, proving that it was N6812.

Little do visitors realise when they look at N6812 in the Imperial War Museum that it is not a Sopwith Camel, but a Dalmuir built Beardmore 2F-1 Ship's Camel, finished to a different standard from any of the other Sopwith Camels. And there it resides to this day far away from its Scottish birthplace, a prize exhibit of a prize aircraft.

(i)

Specification
Type: Single seat scout for Admiralty use
Engine: 150 H.P. Bentley made by Vickers or Humber
Dimensions: Span 26' 11', Length 18' 8", Height 9' 1"

(ii)

Monthly delivery of aeroplanes for Ship's use, Sopwith 2F-1

1917	Aug	Sep	Oct	Nov	Dec	1918	Jan	Feb	Mar
	0	0	0	50	0		0	4	1

(iii)

Sopwith 2F-1 on charge 30 November 1918

2 at contractors and acceptance Parks   109 Grand fleet and Northern Patrol
6 S. E. Area   6 Mediterranean   2 Schools   1 C. T. D.
4 Written off in November

(iv)

Aeroplanes for ship's use, orders from 22 April 1918
[Expected monthly deliveries]

Type	Contractor	Contract	Number on order	Passed to 30. 3. 18	May	Jun	July	Aug	Sept
2F-1	Beardmore	A. S 35920	150		21	30	30	30	14

(v)

Performance of Sopwith 2F-1 Ship Aeroplane
Tested October 1917
Engine: 150 H.P. B.R.1   **Normal B.H.P. at ground level:** 150 at 1250
Lifting surface: 229*   **Speeds**: 108 at 2000', 105.5 at 6500', 103 at 10000'
Endurance: not available   **Service Ceiling**: 17500'
Weight: 1036 empty, 223 fuel/oil, 91 military load, 180 crew [All weights in pounds] *surface of wings

(vi)

Comparative tests of Rotary Engines

Gwynne's 9Z Clerget 1 hour run 24th May 1917
R.P.M: 900   1000   1070   1150   1258
B.H.P: 101.0   110.0   115.3   119.4   123.0
Bore: 120 mm   **Stroke:** 160 mm   **C. R**: 4.26/1
Average B.H.P.:123 **Average R.P.M.:**1252 **B.H.P.** at 1250 R.P.M. 122.8

Bentley A. R.1 1 hour run 22nd May 1917
R.P.M: 912   1024   1110   1206   1310
B.H.P: 111.5   124.5   132.5   139.4   142.6
Bore: 120 mm   **Stroke:** 170 mm   **C. R.** 4.84/1
Average B.H.P.: 137.8 **Average R.P.M.:** 1253 **B.H.P.** at 1250 R.P.M.137.1

(vii)

THE GRAND FLEET
Examples with Beardmore Camels
[Many carried Beardmore Pups and S.B.3d types]

BATTLESHIPS

1. Barham *, Queen Elizabeth, Warspite, Valiant *, Malaya. [Queen Elizabeth Class]
2. Ramillies *, Royal Sovereign, Revenge, Royal Oak [Royal Sovereign Class]
3. Iron Duke, Emperor of India [Iron Duke Class]
4. Conqueror *, Orion [Orion Class]
5. Ajax *, King George V [King George V Class]
6. H.M.S. Canada, H.M.S. Collingwood, H.M.S. Erin

BATTLE CRUISERS

1. Inflexible *, Indomitable * [Invincible Class]
2. Australia *, New Zealand * [Indefatigable Class]
3. Lion *, Princess Royal * [Lion Class]
4. Repulse *, Renown * [Renown Class]
5. H.M.S. Tiger *

LIGHT BATTLE CRUISERS
1. Glorious, Courageous. [Glorious Class]
AIRCRAFT CARRIERS
1. H.M.S. Furious   2. H.M.S. Pegasus*   3. H.M.S. Vindictive 4. H.M.S. Manxman
5. H.M.S. Argus *
CRUISERS
1. H.M.S. Birkenhead, H.M.S. Calliope
2. Dublin *, Chatham, Southampton *, Melbourne, Sydney * [Chatham Class]
3. Weymouth, Yarmouth * [Weymouth Class]
4. Aurora, Phaeton, Royalist *, Penelope, Galatea *, Undaunted *[Arethusa Class]

5. Comus, Cordelia, Caroline [Caroline Class]
6. Caledon, Cassandra [Caledon Class]
7. Dragon, Dauntless [Danae Class]
9. Carlisle, Capetown [Carlisle Class]

DESTROYER
1. H.M.S. Redoubt, with towed lighter
* Clyde Built

(viii)

Examples of Sopwith 2F-1 Camels in Latvian Service

N8137: Built by Hooper & Co., Ltd to contract number 38a/906/c947 & AS37354/18 (BR729) to Latvia 30th January 1919.

N8136: Built by Hooper & Co., Ltd to contract number 38a/906/c947 & AS37354/18 (BR729) to Latvia 30th January 1919.

N8185: Built by Clayton and Shuttleworth ordered 17 May 1918 under contracts, 38a/911/c952, 38a/1153/c1109 & AS 37750/18 (BR738)

N8187: Built by Clayton and Shuttleworth ordered 17 May 1918 under contracts, 38a/911/c952, 38a/1153/c1109 & AS 37750/18 (BR738).

N7143: Built by William Beardmore & Co., Ltd/Arrol Johnston. To Renfrew 28/11/1918, to HMS Vindictive January 1919, tested 10 November 1919 to Latvia.

N8189: Built by Clayton and Shuttleworth ordered 17 May 1918 under contracts, 38a/911/c952, 38a/1153/c1109 & AS 37750/18 (BR738).

N6750: Built by William Beardmore & Co., Ltd, first production model. To HMS Galatea 8th April 1918: to Scapa then Donibristle, then HMS Tiger, 16th January 1919. Transferred around 30 January 1919 to Latvia.

A Latvian 2F-1 Camel

The Handley Page V/1500

The Handley Page V/1500 was Britain's first four engined bomber, designed to fly from the United Kingdom to attack targets on the continent. The decision to go ahead with such an aeroplane was made at an Air Board meeting on 23rd April 1917, but the decision to build was postponed until 30th July, when it was decided to give Handley Page the go - ahead to build three aircraft of an improved type. It was to be a huge aircraft, utilising all the Handley Page experience of its earlier twin engined bombers. The engine installation of the V/1500 was its most important feature; four engines mounted in tandem pairs with one pusher and one tractor engine. The feasibility of this installation had to be tested and one Handley Page 0/100 was selected during October 1917 to prove the idea sound. The designated powerplant was originally the Rolls - Royce Condor, but production of this engine was postponed to rationalise production on the Rolls - Royce Eagle VIII, which ultimately was the standard aero - engine for the V/1500. The decision to proceed with such a radical aircraft was given on the understanding that it would not interrupt the existing aircraft production arrangements.

The design of the bomber was given to Harland and Wolff at Belfast and three prototypes were ordered, designated type "V". During March 1918, William Weir visited the Belfast works and with him was A. J. Campbell, Dalmuir's General Manager. Because of the visit, Beardmore received a contract to build the second order of Handley Page V/1500s to contract number 35A/315/c200, dated 13th March 1918 and confirmed on 2nd April 1918, for twenty aircraft. Beardmore gave this batch the order number 601. At Dalmuir the facilities had the capacity to build fifteen of these huge bombers at a time and no doubt the influence of this made the Air Board decide that Beardmore were to concentrate on bomber production. As an insurance against the failure of Rolls - Royce to supply the Eagle engines the Beardmore Aeroplanes were to standardise on the Galloway Atlantic aero - engine of 500 H.P.

There were great difficulties with the V/1500 programme, not least due to an accident which destroyed the first prototype, but the second prototype flew during the week of 26th July 1918. Beardmore's first bomber, E8287 was completed in June 1918, but it was impossible to fly it out of Dalmuir airfield, so it was taken to Inchinnan and there reassembled for flight. When it was assembled, E8287 had the huge engine radiator built on the fuselage behind the cockpit and a small tail. E8287 took to the air in September 1918 powered by Galloway Atlantics and such was the success of building the "V" bomber that Beardmore received another contract 35A/1662/C1784, for a batch of thirty, with spares for ten. For the Royal Air Force their target was five bombers, three to be powered by Eagles and two to be powered by Atlantics, all to be in service by 1st September 1918. On 14th August 1918, one V/1500 was at the Controller Technical Department to be handed over to General Mullock at Bircham Newton. By the autumn orders had been received by the contractors for 255 aircraft, but by the end of October 1918 only three were ready for service. By then all the Beardmore aeroplanes had had their engines standardised on the Rolls - Royce Eagle, with production of the Galloway Atlantic being allowed to lapse. On the night of the 10th November 1918, the V/1500 was being readied for raids on Berlin, but technical difficulties with the engines meant that the raid never took place and was cancelled with the Armistice. By the end of 1918 thirty V/1500s had been built and, even with the Armistice, production was allowed to continue. The fourth Beardmore V/1500 completed its trials at Inchinnan on Friday 16th May 1919 and was delivered to Folkestone the next day flown by Clifford Prodger. The fifth bomber was completed on 28th May 1919 and flown south again by Clifford Prodger. On 16th June 1919, Prodger collected E8291 and flew it south, down the East Coast to Folkestone, without any hitches at all, the whole trip taking six hours. During the flight, Prodger had to leave the cockpit to check the mechanics at the fuel tanks. There he found them sound asleep. Beardmore "V" bombers had detailed differences from other production machines especially round the nose, but generally they were similar to production models. The production target was one per month. According to the Ministry of Munitions records, Dalmuir completed seven out of the fifty bombers ordered. The cancellation and liquidation of these contracts was investigated by the Commons Select Committee on National Expenditure, which wanted to know the policy of the Ministry of Munitions on this matter.

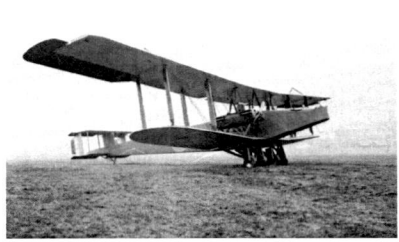
An 0/400 with tandem engines for test

V/1500 cockpit pilot to the right

Eagle engines installed

V/1500 with Galloway Atlantics

A V/1500 at Inchinnan before delivery flight

A V/1500 bomber being readied for flight in late 1918

Beardmore V/1500 at Bircham Newton

V/1500 in flight

Prodger in the centre with Frederick Handley Page and the 40 passengers

The policy was clear; that the most modern types, such as the V/1500, were to remain in production, while the older types were to be withdrawn. Most V/1500s were never accepted by the Royal Air Force, being flown to such places as Folkestone (Hawkinge) and there dismantled.

In production the V/1500 was dogged by shortages, principally of spruce and experiments were made at Dalmuir replacing the wooden wing main spars with metal spars made of duralumin. Vibration problems with the initial engine fit of Galloway Atlantics was traced to the propellers and new ones were manufactured to cure the problem. The propeller combination was two blades at the front with four blades at the rear, but at Inchinnan, two blades were tried front and rear. At 92 M.P.H., the V/1500 could carry a crew of six, thirty 250 lb. bombs, machine guns and other supplies and with the load smaller, it could fly 1200 miles. The designated bombs were the 520 lb. light case and the 550 lb. heavy case, with both being developed in the early months of 1918. In addition, experiments were carried out with bombs weighing 1400 lbs., 1600 lbs. and the SN 1700 lb. The Handley Page had the capacity to carry 16000 six and a half ounce incendiary bomblets, with one intention, to set Berlin ablaze. The Independent Air Force had carried out trials for this in the late summer of 1918, when they bombed the Black Forest. If the war had lasted into the spring of 1919, the Royal Air Force would have had eight squadrons of the V/1500 based in Britain (Bircham Newton) and others in France, at Nancy. The aircraft park was to be at St. Blin, which had two airfields, east and west and was a combined United States Air Service Depot A.E.F. with the Independent Air Force. One V/1500 made its way to India and there it was used to bomb the Afghan rebels. In Afghanistan, the rebels called it, "The mother of all aeroplanes,", but to the Royal Air Force it was, "The Bloody Paralyser." After the end of the war, the Handley Page pilot Clifford Prodger flew in a V/1500 with forty passengers over London then he returned to America. When Prodger was flying a Bristol Fighter in California, the aircraft broke up in the air and he was killed. In January 1919, St Blin in the upper Marne was returned to agriculture, never achieving the status of a night-bomber, aircraft park or base. The Handley Page V/1500 was a triumph for the British aircraft industry. It took eleven months to build and fly from the initial design stage in 1917 to the first flight of the prototype in May 1918. Who could imagine that Dalmuir would mass-produce one of Britain's first warplanes, the B.E 2c and culminate their aviation skills with that supreme aero - product of the Great War, the Handley Page V/1500.

(i)
Specification

Engines: Rolls - Royce Eagle Eights or Galloway Atlantics
Dimensions: Span 126' 0", Length 64' 0", Height 23' 0"
Endurance: 12/14 hours **Speed:** 99 M.P.H. at 6500'

(ii)
Performance of V/1500

Tested -/9/18 at Martlesham Heath Report No. 228
Seats: 6 **Engines:** 4 R/R Eagles **Rate of climb:** 450 ft./min.
Ceiling: 12800' **Useful Load:** 8490 lbs. **Speed:** 97 M.P.H. at 8750'
Engine Nos.: F.P. 8/Eagle/1866   F.S. 8/Eagle/1810
             R.P. 8/Eagle/1826   R.S. 8/Eagle/1792
Climbing trial carried out with the following loads.

Crew of 6	1080lbs
Deadweight	3120lbs
Petrol 515 gallons	3670lbs
Oil 64 gallons	620lbs
Total weight of machine	24700lbs
Weight of machine bare (with water)	16210lbs
Area of main planes (including ailerons)	2896 sq. feet

Span 125' 6" **Height** 22' 0" **Length** 64' 4" **R.P.M.** at 97 M.P.H. **F.P.** 1800 **R.P.** 1810 **F.S.** 1815 **R.S.** 1785

A V/1500 beside the hangar and an example with wings folded

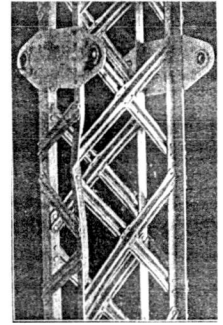 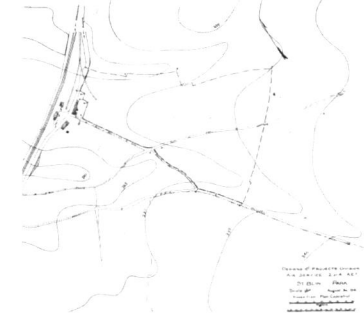

V/1500 metal wing spar USAS/IAF base at St Blin designed for the V/1500

The prototype V/1500 with enclosed engine cowlings

Clifford Prodger and passenger on final delivery of a Beardmore V/1500

W. B. IIb

The genealogy of this aeroplane can be traced back to an adaptation of the B.E 2c, the W.B. II. The W.B IIb was designed as a fast mail plane in order to attract government contracts for airmail flights. Originally conceived around the B.H.P. engine of 1916 as a fighter reconnaissance biplane, the W.B. IIb was reworked as a mail plane around the 160 H.P. Beardmore aero - engine. It had a range of 415 miles with this powerplant, or 361 miles with the 200 H.P. version and work commenced on two aircraft in 1919. As the W.B. IIb these two aeroplanes were fitted with the 160 H.P. Beardmore, the first production model flying to Cricklewood in November 1920. The second machine was displayed at the Olympia Air Show in July 1920 and flew the first commercial flight from Renfrew to Croydon in September 1920. On this occasion, Captain Charles Ward who had come from Blackburn Aircraft flew it. One is reported as having crashed in Huntington during a proving flight.

Due to the supply of more modern designs from the Aircraft Disposal Company the design of the W.B.IIb came to nothing. Charles Ward went to South America and flew in Venezuela. He then taught Spanish officers to fly the DH9. He also flew as a pioneer with Alan Cobham's Flight Refuelling Company and then returned to Blackburn Aircraft.

Specification
Type: Two seat passenger transport or single - seat mailplane
Engine: 160 H.P. Beardmore
Speed: 107 M.P.H. at sea level
Dimensions: Span: 35' 0", Length: 27' 7", Height: 10' 11"

G-EARY on display at Olympia

Captain Ward with the IIb at Renfrew

W.B.IX

In 1920 G.T. Richards designed a ten-seat amphibian biplane for an Air Ministry competition, which was to be powered by Beardmore aero - engines of 200 H.P (Adriatic's). The engines were installed in the hull and drove the propellers through a system of drives and couplings through the fuselage. The pilot sat above the hull and the tail was attached to the hull by two outriggers. There were two cabins in the hull with four large portholes to increase passenger view. The hull was layered with mahogany, while the hull framework was made of duralumin. The W.B. IX could land on an aerodrome or be wheeled up a slipway to be serviced. It had a crew of two with a capacity for ten passengers. Unfortunately this design was never completed and the airframe was scrapped at Dalmuir with the closure of the Beardmore Aviation Department.

Specification
Type: Ten seater passenger amphibian
Engines: Four 200 H.P. Beardmore aero - engines
Speed: 93 M.P.H.
Dimensions: Length: 62' 0" Span: 107" 0", Height: 20' 6"

An impression of the WBIX, it was 90% complete when work was stopped

W.B. X

The design of the W.B. X appears to be an amalgam of some of the features of the W.B.II, the D.F.W. and the W.B. IV. It was built for an Air Ministry competition. The fuselage was streamlined and of circular cross - section. The pilot sat towards the rear with the passenger inside the fuselage at the front, enclosed by a Triplex roof. Access for the passenger was by a ladder, which fitted over the engine exhaust. For its time the W.B. X had one unique feature; it was one of the first all - metal aeroplanes to be built in Britain. All the wooden parts had been replaced with duralumin pieces, which had been cast from the original wooden aircraft parts and it utilised all the Beardmore experience in the building of airships. As such, it was the only one of its kind built at Dalmuir. Shorts had built the "Silver Streak", but the duralumin was so unstable that it was felt to be unsafe to fly and it was scrapped after only two flights. After being flown on its initial trial at Martlesham Heath in August 1920, the W.B. X was scrapped after only one flight, the duralumin having deteriorated to such an extent that the aircraft was dangerous. Power was provided by the 160 or 200 H.P. Beardmore aero – engine. This was the last design G.T. Richards was involved in at Dalmuir.

Specification
Type: Two seat passenger aircraft
Engine: 160 or 200 H.P. Beardmore
Speed: 91 or 97 M.P.H. at sea level
Dimensions: Length: 26' 0", Span: 46' 0", Height: 11' 10"

The WBX being readied for flight at Martlesham Heath

W.B. XXIV

One of the most pleasant designs worked on in 1919 was a single seat all - metal biplane tourer. It was to be powered by a five-cylinder radial engine, but was modified to take a two-cylinder powerplant. As such it was called the Beardmore W.B. VIc. The concept of a single engined tourer lay dormant until 1924 when W. S. Shackleton took over the design. With the impetus of another Air Ministry competition Shackleton re-designed the W.B. VIc around the 32 H.P. Bristol Cherub two cylinders aero - engine. This aeroplane was to be called the W. B. XXIV or "Wee Bee" and was built entirely of wood. One of its important features was the design of its box wing, which was built up of wooden laminations around a box structure. Although this made the W.B.XXIV very strong it also made it extremely expensive to build. It could carry a pilot and one passenger. The W.B. XXIV was test flown at Renfrew aerodrome where it was found to be a delight to fly. It was extremely pleasant in the air, with well – balanced, crisp controls. It was entered for the 1924 light aeroplane competition at Lympne and though there were some difficulties with the Bristol Cherub (it threw a small end on one piston) it won the competition. This gave W. S. Shackleton the unique position of having designed two entries for the competition, the other aeroplane being the A.N.E.C.

Only one "Wee Bee" was built and it never progressed from its initial win at Lympne, since it was a much more expensive aeroplane to build and run. De Havilland went on to produce the two - seat Moth that was to dominate the British civil scene for the next three decades. There was no demand for the W.B. XXIV. When W. S. Shackleton moved to Australia the Wee Bee followed and flew there until 1939. It is known to have existed there to at least 1949, when Vincent Boyes in Victoria owned it. It was put up for sale in December 1951 at a price of £125, with the Cherub having only one hour on the clock, but nothing is known of its fate.

Specification

Type: Two seat tourer or trainer
Engine: 32 H.P. Bristol Cherub
Speed: 87 M.P.H. **Dimensions:** Length: 22' 2", Span: 48' 10", Height: 4' 10"

The Wee Bee at the competition   In Australia where it did not survive

W.B. XXVI

The W. B. XXVI was a high-speed two-seat fighter powered by the 375 H.P. Rolls-Royce Eagle IX aero - engine and was first flown in 1925. The aircraft was built entirely of wood with fabric covering. Unusually for those times, as a biplane, it lacked any flying or landing wires and could be dismantled and reassembled in minutes. The undercarriage could take severe punishment and the aeroplane could be taxied above 50 M.P.H. over the roughest terrain. The armament of the W.B.XXVI consisted of three Beardmore - Farquhar machine guns, two firing through the propeller and one for the observer. It was built for the Latvian Government, who had displayed an interest in the design. Squadron Leader de Haga Haig had toured extensively in the Baltic advertising Beardmore products and had attracted the Latvian interest. At its first demonstration to the public at Renfrew aerodrome in December 1925 the W.B. XXVI was dived and looped at over 200 M.P.H.

Interest from Latvia waned after only three flights and only the single machine was built. It existed until at least 1928, but then its fate is obscure. The Royal Air Force showed no interest in the design because it was constructed totally of wood, an obsolete material in their eyes and powered by an engine at the end of its life. Besides, Hawkers were on the verge of producing the Hart family of two seat general-purpose aeroplanes. With no Air Ministry orders forthcoming, there was no demand for the last W. S. Shackleton, Beardmore design and the aircraft disappeared into obscurity.

Specification

Type: Two seat fighter
Engine: Rolls - Royce Eagle or Napier Lion
Speed: 145 M.P.H. at sea level
Dimensions: Span: 37" 0" [top], 32' 0" [bottom], Length: 27' 10"

The W.B.XXVI at Renfrew

The gunner's cupola with the B/F MG

Beardmore – Rohrbach

The construction of the all - metal Inverness flying boats and the single Inflexible trimotor monoplane at Dalmuir was part of the Air Ministry's concerted investigation into metal wings and all - metal aeroplanes. Shortage of aviation materials, principally wood, at the closing stages of the Great War, led the Air Ministry into a series of trials with all - metal components in aeroplanes. Vickers was the main British firm that led in this field. They had tested metal parts on the Vickers Vimy bomber and built the all - metal wings for an Avro 504 at Barrow. During this 1918-19 period Beardmore were pioneering all metal wing construction on the Handley - Page V/1500 bomber, but the real pioneers were the Germans. During the war they had experienced greater wood shortages than the British had and had started to concentrate heavily on the construction of all - metal aeroplanes. There were two German firms pioneering with all - metal construction, Junkers and Zeppelin, the airship firm. One of the Zeppelin designers was Claude Dornier who began to build a series of seaplanes using light - weight airship metal. The first Dornier designed seaplane took off from Lake Constance during 1916. Helping Claude Dornier with his work was Adolf Karl Rohrbach who had joined the Zeppelin firm from the shipbuilding firm of Blohm and Voss in 1914. In 1917, Rohrbach was transferred from Zeppelin work to the Staaken plant as a designer. At the Berlin Staaken Zeppelin works the Germans were building four - engined bombers with one aim in mind, to bomb London.

In 1919, after the Armistice, Rohrbach became the chief designer at Staaken and started work on a large four - engined civil transport [the E4/24 project] to be called "Staaken." Due to the terms of the Armistice the Staaken had to be scrapped under the orders of the Allied powers. This ban on German aeroplane production led Dornier producing his own aircraft in Italy and another German aircraft builder, Ernst Heinkel, building in Sweden. In 1922 Adolf Rohrbach founded his own company, Rohrbach Metallflugzeugbau GmbH in Berlin, with the branch assembly plant in Denmark. That year Rohrbach received a contract from the Japanese government to build the Rohrbach Ro II. These were delivered on the 11th November 1923 with four more in 1925. There they were known as the Mitsubishi Type R. The components for all the Rohrbach aeroplanes were made in Berlin, then taken by rail to Copenhagen. While Rohrbach was developing his business, the British Air Ministry was also taking an active interest in all - metal aeroplanes. In the post - war period the Royal Air Force had to rely on wooden hulled wartime flying boats for fishery protection and coastal patrol and these aeroplanes had to have a high degree of servicing. From July 1921 to February 1923 ten flying boats had been built for the Royal Air Force and as they were delivered scrapping of the old stock of flying boats had commenced.

The Air Ministry had also adopted the policy of ordering one metal aeroplane order for every experimental order of aircraft. These experimental contracts were placed at a time when the British aircraft industry lacked fresh orders because of the vast stock of wartime aeroplanes that were remaining. During 1923 one contract was placed with William Beardmore & Co., Ltd., at Dalmuir, for an all - metal civil aeroplane with an initial cost of £12400. It was a high winged monoplane powered by three Rolls - Royce Condors and with a reported capacity of twenty passengers. Local firms benefited from this order, the major supplier of duralumin being the Clyde Alloy Steel Company and the first orders were placed with them during 1923. This machine was regarded as a joint Anglo - German project, with both firms having an equal share. Rohrbach called this giant civil airliner the Be - Ro, <u>B</u>eardmore and <u>R</u>ohrbach, BE-RO 1, but to William Beardmore & Co., Ltd., it became AV 1, the Beardmore Inflexible.

N183 on delivery at Felixtowe and being prepared for flight in Denmark

Rohrbach wings being constructed at Dalmuir also showing wing bulkhead

Interior of the Inverness

The tail of Inverness N183 in Denmark

The Rohrbach flying boat in sail

N184 on delivery over Kilcreggan

Beardmore Inflexible at Martlesham Heath where it was assembled

The size of the Inflexible can be clearly seen in relation to the Dunlop wheels

On 21st December 1922 Alan Chorlton, the firm's chief engineer, had submitted a patent for a box girder wing, stiffened with angles and channels, made of aluminium or magnesium. This patent was accepted on 21st March 1924. One month later, Adolf Rohrbach applied for his patent of a box wing structure that was accepted on 9th July 1925. Rohrbach had covered extensively all of his designs with patents, including tail, rudder, undercarriage and even his unique sail arrangement for his flying boats. Rohrbach had called his use of the cantilever design principle in his wings and aircraft structure, "stress skin construction." To demonstrate the strength of his wing design and construction, Rohrbach had sixteen men walk along one wing without doing any damage. Even with having W. S. Shackleton as a designer, whose experience was working on wing structures, Beardmore adopted the Rohrbach system of construction. But with that came a penalty. A royalty had to be paid to Rohrbach for the use of his patents and in one year £9000 was paid out in fees.

In addition to the AV 1 order for the Inflexible, Beardmore had to supply the Royal Air Force with two additional all - metal flying boats and these were given the constructor's number AV 5, to be called Inverness. The first flying boat was sent from Denmark to the test centre at Felixstowe on 18th September 1925. This two-year delay was probably due to finalising the patent fees and royalties. This first Inverness cost £6134: 15s: 6d and that included spares. The identity of this Inverness in the Rohrbach number system is not clear, but it was probably a Ro IIIa flying boat. When it was inspected at Felixstowe it was found to have more in common with bridge - building techniques than with aircraft construction. The hull used riveted duralumin panels built up on plates and bulkheads (like a ship) and was immensely strong. The wings of this cantilever monoplane had no ribs, but the skin was supported at intervals by vertical panels. Power was supplied by two Rolls - Royce Eagle engines mounted above the fuselage, with the floats being carried close to the centre line. It was said to be extremely pleasant to fly. Dr. Rohrbach had evolved a system of anti - corrosion treatment for his all - metal aircraft. It consisted of spraying all the metal components with a layer of zinc. Beardmore had noticed this as a sales point, claiming that the Inverness could be left out for months on end without any deterioration in structure. Unfortunately, they were wrong. All these points were what the Air Ministry wanted to investigate, but the Master of Semphill, who was in charge of the test programme, said that the tests were to be completed as quickly as possible. He also added another sentiment, "We have no faith in monoplanes." When in service the Inverness 1, now serialled N183 was a very complicated machine to keep serviceable. There were problems with the fuel supply, wing flexing and engine maintenance. Looking at the aeroplanes of those times, wooden biplanes, it is not surprising that the existence of such a modern type would cause maintenance problems.

 The Inverness 1 had poor sea keeping qualities. It was unusual, even among Rohrbach designs, in having a flat-bottomed hull towards the nose. This would make taking off and landing in the sea an extremely difficult undertaking. More problems arose; water penetration and corrosion around the wing roots at the fuselage, tail vibration at speed and on one occasion the flying boat hull collapsed at the step. The major airframe repairs were carried out by Beardmore and in 1926 they supplied further Inverness spares to Air Ministry contract S/890/1/2/3. This experience in Rohrbach construction had a side benefit for Beardmore. They were able to supply components to Rohrbach at Copenhagen for the parent company's further designs.

 While experiments were being carried out on the Beardmore Inverness the Air Ministry were actively investigating other all - metal aircraft. They purchased from Germany an all - metal Junkers F13, a Dornier Delphin and a Heinkel. They were also doing comparison trials into the German aircraft wing sections, which were designed to

Gottingen specifications, and the R. A. F. 15 wing section. The British wing was found to be superior. At Dalmuir, work was progressing slowly on the Inflexible. This was due to the complexity of the design, the nature of the materials used and the size of the work force. Some of the expertise came from Germany, but its unique braking system came from Automotive Products and was designed along the lines of a motor car. It was planned that when the tail wheel touched the ground the brakes would come into operation automatically and slows the aeroplane down. So slow was its construction that it took four years to build, 1923 to 1927 and because of this the all - metal experimental programme became the subject of Parliamentary questions. The Air Minister refused to take any questions on the giant three engined, all - metal, civil airliner declaring, "It was against the public interest." By the 24th November 1926 the minister, in reply to a Parliamentary question, said the aeroplane had not been delivered and declined to mention costs. The Inflexible was delivered to Air Ministry contract AM S213 costing £2198: 15s: 5d. It had to be delivered by sea from Dalmuir to Ipswich Docks in sections due to its size. Owing to the secrecy of the contract it was given a civil registration as a cover, G-EBNG and few details of its existence were made public. The "Times" reported that it had been delivered in the middle of 1927 (July) and when assembled it had to be built and rebuilt many times. This is confirmed in "Flight" for November 1927. The Inflexible was ready for its first flight on 5th March 1928 with Squadron Leader Noakes at the controls and a Beardmore mechanic as a passenger. Both wore parachutes. On its first flight it took off on a very short run, then Noakes flew around for fifteen minutes at 2000 feet and when he landed he described the Inflexible as a pilot's aeroplane. In conjunction with Noakes as test pilot was Squadron Leader de Haga Haig, with both flying the Inflexible between 1928 and 1929. At the Norwich display of 1929 the pilot was told not to do any aerobatics, proving that size was not against the design. When its test flying phase was completed the engines were removed and the hulk used for anti - corrosion tests with paints. The structure was then tested to destruction when a series of weights was placed along the aeroplane until the metal structure broke. What was left of the airframe lasted into 1931 at Martlesham Heath then it quietly disappeared.

The final aeroplane in the all-metal trio was the Dalmuir built Beardmore Inverness N184, which was possibly a Rohrbach RO IV. Again this machine was hand finished throughout. In comparison to the earlier machine there were many design changes. Principally it was the engine installation, Napier lions replacing the Rolls Royce Eagles and the side floats being placed differently in relation to the fuselage. Much of the design detail changes were completed to the plans of H.J.Steiger and Rollo de Haga Haig, these changes being tested in a model at Farnborough. N184 was lowered into the Clyde on 28th November 1928 and the awkwardness of its size meant the dockyard crane could not be used and a substitute was used instead. The pilot for the Inverness on its maiden flight was Squadron Leader Rea who had once flown the Beardmore Farquhar equipped Bristol Fighter on 17th November 1919. Once in the water the Inverness was taken all the way up the Clyde, past Bowling, Dumbarton and Helensburgh, to be moored in the Gareloch. From there it was flown out of Scotland to Felixstowe on 30th November 1928. There it was poorly received. It was felt that it was a worse machine than Inverness 1, N183 and during 1929 Felixstowe reported that it would not be worthwhile carrying out any more trials or performance tests. Both aircraft were quickly broken up in what would be today regarded as a limited test period. Rohrbach felt the design still had some life in it and projected a fourteen-seat airliner. The side floats could be removed and wheels installed, but this idea came to nothing. In 1926 Dr. A. Rohrbach travelled extensively in the United States, lecturing on his method of aeroplane construction. There were many listeners including Donald Douglas and Jack Northrop. From then on all American aeroplanes were built of stressed skin metal construction and they still are to this day.

In Germany, due to the economic climate, there was an end to state subsidy and with this came an increase in financial liabilities for many companies, including Rohrbach Aircraft. During 1929 Adolf Rohrbach sold his company to Weserflugzeugbau GmbH and he became their technical director and designer. This company produced little in the way of innovative aeroplane construction being used as a sub - contract firm for the Focke - Wulf Company. The war years and the ensuing destruction of Germany were never witnessed by Adolf

Karl Rohrbach for, while on holiday in Kampen in the Isle of Sylt in April 1939, he suddenly died and the world lost one of its great aircraft pioneers

Inverness

Specification
Type: Twin engined flying boat
Engines: Two rolls Royce Eagles or Napier Lions
Speed: 110 M.P.H. at sea level

Dimensions: Span: 90' 0", Length: 56' 0", Height: 16' 3", Wing area: 756 sq. ft.
Weight: 1330 lbs. [Source Air Ministry]

Inflexible

Specification
Type: Large Research Aircraft
Engines: Three Rolls - Royce Condors
Speed: 110 M.P.H. at sea level

Dimensions: Span 147' 0", Length 75' 6", Height 21' 0", Wing area 1936 sq. ft.
Weight: 31400 lbs. [Source Squadron Leader Rollo de Haga Haig]

Another view of the Inflexible on display showing the panels wrinkling

AERO-ENGINES

The Austro-Daimler series at Arrol Johnston
The evolution of the BHP at Galloway Motors
The airship engines at Parkhead
Loss of airship R101

AUSTRO – DAIMLER

The great problem for British aeroplane manufacturers in the early part of twentieth century was simply that no satisfactory British aero - engine had been developed for aircraft use. The British Government had recognised this and in April 1912 Colonel Seely published his Parliamentary report into the situation. Among his recommendations was that the British try to perfect a satisfactory aero - engine for aircraft use and if necessary try to import the licence to produce them. Foreign aero- engine manufacturers saw little business prospects in this country and were hostile to any requests for technical information. At that time no less than fifteen manufactures had been approached. By August 1913 these efforts by official pressure were beginning to show results. British manufacturers had obtained foreign engines and were in the process of obtaining licences to manufacture them in this country, some to be used in the aero - engine competitions set by the British Government for 1914.

    At its annual general meeting on the 17th November 1913, William Beardmore & Co., Ltd. ratified the licence agreement for the 120 H.P. Austro - Daimler engine, an engine that was German in origin. This engine had successfully powered S. F. "Colonel" Cody's aircraft to first place in the British Military Reliability Tests of August 1912. It had also gained honours when it powered the Martynside Monoplane to second place out of eleven competitors at the Second Aerial Derby in September 1913. The Austro - Daimler was a six cylinder, water cooled in line power plant and was regarded as ideal for licence production, having gained many international records to its credit. In 1911 it had gained nine world records through, speed, distance and time trials and, by 1912, had gained four awards for altitude, including one for vertical speed. During 1913 its passenger carrying abilities were proven, when awards for duration and height were gained for carrying an average of five passengers. For the production of the Austro - Daimler, Beardmore formed a company called "Beardmore Austro Daimler Ltd." on the 25th July 1913. The majority of the shares were held by Beardmore, but William Beardmore held one share to qualify as a director. Production of the aero - engine was to be entrusted to Arrol - Johnston at Dumfries, who manufactured motor - cars, a firm that was wholly owned by William Beardmore. In January 1914 the original British Austro - Daimler Company offered three sizes of aero - engine for aeroplane installation, a four cylinder 65 H.P. model and two six cylinder models of 90 H.P. and 120 H.P. All were of the vertical in - line type with water cooling, utilising Austro - Daimler radiators in three sizes, 40 lbs., 53 lbs. and 62 lbs. for their respective engine type. Each engine type was fitted with a self - starter and in case of starting malfunctions a starting handle was provided. By March 1914 Beardmore had finally taken over the Austro - Daimler concession in Britain and were exhibiting at Olympia. At the exhibition the 90 H.P. and the 120 H.P. were put on show, but the 65 h. p was not displayed. The 90 H.P. model had been used by Sopwith to power the Sopwith Bat Boat and had been thoroughly tested and proven.

    The Austrian Army had taken a 90 H.P. engine and tested it over a twenty - four hour period at full throttle, with a propeller being directly attached to the engine. After the test the engine was dismantled, weighed, measured and thoroughly inspected and it was found to be in perfect condition. The 120 H.P. Beardmore engine was redesigned from the original Austro - Daimler in some detail; to avoid distortion, the cylinders were machined inside and out and were attached to the crank - case by seven hold down bolts. The valve mechanism was of the Porsche system of patented rocking lever, operated by single push rods through the crank - case. Lubrication was by Bosch, which was claimed gave a pressure of 1000 lbs. per square inch. Modifications were also made to the carburettor and ignition system, all with the object of increasing reliability, cutting down servicing and eliminating breakdowns. S. F. Cody had proved the reliability of the original Austro - Daimler when he flew it over a twelve month period without it being overhauled.

Shortly after Beardmore took over Austro - Daimler in this country the War Office ordered twenty four 120 H.P. engines to power the R.E. 5. These aeroplanes were bought with the £25000 paid to the War Office by the Admiralty when the latter took over all the Army airships in 1913. When the Great War broke out in August 1914, Beardmore Austro - Daimler Aero - Engine Ltd. changed its name on the 13th October 1914 to "Beardmore Aero - Engines Ltd." and the R.E. 5 flew with Beardmore aero - engines in France during 1914 - 15. There they performed yeoman service, even being involved in an operation which resulted in the pilot receiving the Victoria Cross [V.C.]. The R.E. 5 was redesigned into the R.E. 7, powered by the next engine in the series the 160 H.P. Beardmore and it only equipped one squadron of the R.F.C, No. 21. The R.E.7 was in service until August 1916 when it was replaced by the B.E. 12, but it did serve throughout the Battle of the Somme in July 1916. One R.E. 7, powered by the 120 H.P. Beardmore, was fitted with one of the first engine superchargers at Farnborough in September 1915, when 2348 was fitted with a Blower R. A. E. no II. This was a centrifugal blower and it boosted up the ground level condition to 6000', so that power did not drop off as the aeroplane climbed. It was fitted with a slipping clutch to relieve shocks and it had an independent petrol pump. The same blower was fitted to a B.E 2c fitted with a 150 H.P. Hispano Engine, but that was some months later. As the war progressed, the Beardmore powered R.E. 7 was relegated to target towing and training.

At Arrol - Johnston the War Office had posted in its own inspector from the Aeronautical Inspection Directorate. His job was to speed up production and see that any modifications carried out to the engines were up to standard. The inspector at Dumfries was Frank Halford, who had been commissioned into the R.F.C in the autumn of 1914, his commission being gazetted in February 1915. When Austro - Daimler agreed to set up production in Britain many of its technicians were sent to help with the production line. Unfortunately for them, when the war broke out they were interned.

While working in the Royal Aircraft Factory in 1914 Geoffrey de Havilland designed a pusher biplane around the 120 H.P. engine. This aeroplane was the D. H. 1, but due to production difficulties with the

120 H.P. engine, it had to be fitted with the 70 H.P. Renault. Even this obsolete aeroplane remained in production until at least 1917 with thirty eight D. H.1as remaining on order. Early in 1916 Airco proposed the D. H.3 around the 120 H.P. Engine, but in a pusher form. As a twin engined fighter the D. H.3 was a failure and it was redesigned as the D. H. 10 in a much more conventional form with the engines mounted as tractors on the wings. Another firm which saw the potential of the 120 H.P. Beardmore was the Bristol & Colonial Company, which had designed an aeroplane around two 150 H.P. R. A. F.a engines. Unavailability of these engines meant the 120 H.P. engine was used instead. The Bristol T. T. [for Twin Tractor] was flown during May 1916, but performance of the two prototypes was way below expectation. Its average speed was 62 M.P.H., so the type was abandoned. When the designated aero - engine became available the D. H. 1 became the D. H.1a and was used in the Middle - East for escort and patrol. As a two seater it followed the current fashion of placing the gunner at the nose with the pilot at the rear.

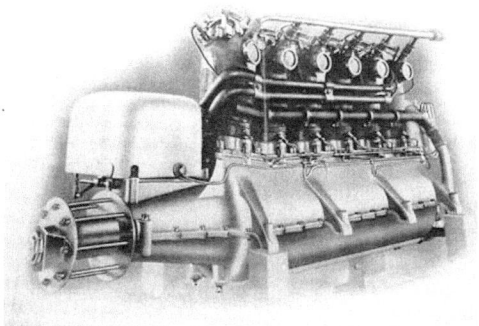 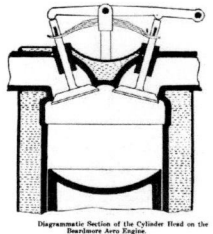

The original Austro-Daimler   Valve arrangement

The Beardmore aero-engine

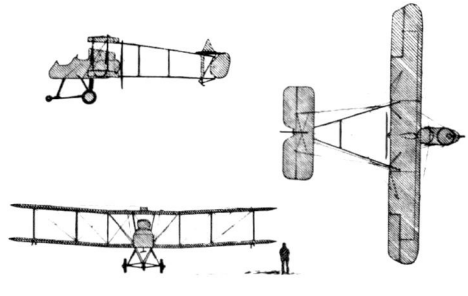

The F.E. 2b

Weir built F.E.2b A5666 at Renfrew

Martinsyde Scout

   Another company which took an interest in the 120 H.P. Beardmore was Martynside. During 1915 they designed a large two bay; single seat biplane designated the G100 around the 120 H.P. Beardmore. Powered by Engine No. 302, with a three bladed propeller the prototype, 4735, was tested at Upavon in September 1915. The G100 was accepted for service and served with 27 Squadron in Mesopotamia and Palestine where it was used with other mixed squadrons as a fighter escort. It was a large aeroplane and was more the size of a bomber than a fighter. As the war progressed, Arrol - Johnston modified the 120 H.P. Beardmore by enlarging the bore from 130 mm to 142 mm, which is a normal modification to get more power from a piston - engine. This new aero - engine was called the,

"160 H.P. Beardmore", but due to production difficulties, only two had been produced by the spring of 1916. Many of the working detail parts were interchangeable with the 120 H.P. engine such as the centres and sizes of the hold down bolts of the cylinder blocks. This meant that both engines could be fitted into the engine bay of the same aeroplane without modification. Martynside used this property to good effect when they fitted the 160 H.P. Beardmore to the G100, which then became the G102. This version of the Martynside was universally known to the R.F.C. as the Martynside "Elephant" and when flown at 6500' the G102 had a maximum speed of 102 M.P.H. which was 7 M.P.H. faster than the G100. In comparison with the earlier version the G102 had an endurance of five and a half hours, which was an hour better than the G100. In an effort to increase the armament of the G 102 from one Lewis gun, a similar weapon was fitted to port behind the pilot. The use of this modification to the armament must have been physically trying for the pilot as he had to turn and physically aim the weapon. The 120 H.P. was also designed around a two seat fighter called the R2A which was the product of Bristol and Colonial Aircraft's designer, Frank Barnwell. Unavailability of the 120 H.P. meant that a newer engine of the Rolls Royce type was chosen for the R2A and what resulted was probably the finest two seater of its time, the Bristol Fighter.

One of the most unusual types of Beardmore powered aeroplanes was the Norman Thomson N. T.2b flying boat trainer of which more than 150 were built for both the R.N.A.S. and R.F.C. Another type was the White and Thomson No. 3 flying boat, of which three were built, serving with the R.N.A.S. in 1915. The 120 H.P. Beardmore also inspired one of the truly great aeroplanes of the Great War, the Armstrong Whitworth F. K. 8. Popularly known as the "Big Ack" and designed by the Dutchman Frederick Koolhoven, it first flew in May 1916 and was used for reconnaissance duties with the R.F.C. in France and Italy. With a wing span of forty three feet six inches and a crew of two, the first F. K. 8s had their radiators mounted as a Vee ahead of the pilot on struts. As the war progressed the radiators were mounted on either side of the fuselage and the nose contours were modified. The unusual radiator installation was investigated and it was found that to get cooling for the engine there was no practical difference to where the radiators were fitted. Throughout the war the A.W.F.K. 8 flew with fuselage radiators. The A.W.F.K. 8 arrived in France with 35 Squadron in January 1917 and earned an excellent reputation for engine reliability and handling qualities. An unusual feature was the provision of a second set of pilot's controls in the air gunner's cockpit, which was used to good effect on at least two occasions. The pilot of one, 2nd Lieutenant McLeod and his observer Lt. A.W. Hammond were attacked by Fokker Triplanes. Hammond shot down one, but they were then attacked by seven more. After destroying two, the aeroplane caught fire and the petrol tank exploded. The heat from the fire was so intense that McLeod left the cockpit and standing on the wing he side slipped the A.W.F.K. 8 with one hand on the control column and force landed. Later they were rescued by British troops.

On the 10th August 1918, an A.W.F.K. 8 was flying at about 1500' when the crew saw a large concentration of enemy troops. Captain West, with his observer Haslam, flew low over the site of a wood three times to confirm their position. Then they were attacked by a German fighter which pressed home its attack with accurate fire. In the ensuing battle West's leg was shot off, the aircraft crashed, with both crew being rescued by Canadian troops. Before going to hospital Captain West insisted on making his report. For their gallantry the pilots of both A.W.F.K. 8s received the Victoria Cross.

Production of the A.W.F.K. 8 was to continue until the autumn of 1918, when it was due to be replaced by a version of the Bristol Fighter with the Sunbeam Arab engine. Of a total of 1500 built some 725 were on charge at the war's end, with fifty being written off. The other major users of both the 120 and 160 H.P. Beardmore engines were the F. E.2a and F. E.2b, both having been designed at the Royal Aircraft Factory, Farnborough. The F. E.2a was designed during 1914 and, for ease of production, shared the outer wing panels with the B.E 2c. Twelve were ordered off the drawing board, but were to be powered by the Green engine in pusher form, with the first one flying on the 26th January 1915. The Green engine was a failure and the 120 H.P. Beardmore was fitted as a substitute, with the new prototype flying in April 1915. By June 1915 five F. E.2a s were based in France, where they were used by 6 Squadron. It was at their base, Abeele, near Ypres, that the first night - flying bombing trials were carried out, pioneering techniques used later in the war. The F. E.2b was a much simpler aeroplane to produce than the F. E.2a, but when it first flew it was fitted with the 120 H.P. engine. Later the 160 H.P. Beardmore was substituted and the first one to fly with this engine was 6357, with engine No. 600, during February 1916. Resembling a large bird cage the "Fee" was instrumental in crushing the German Fokker monoplanes in France and in fact was deadlier than the much more conventionally designed Sopwith Strutter. The gunner sat at the front of the nose and had a tremendous field of fire and in some versions of the F. E.2b a Lewis gun was fitted to a post in front of the pilot helping the gunner to fire over the top wing. When attacked, the "Fee" formed a circle with others of its type, making it very difficult to penetrate or be shot down. With the arrival of more modern types later in the war it would have seemed that the F. E.2b would have been relegated to second line duties, but this was not the case. By August 1917 it was being used for ground attack and night bombing, both the F. E.2a and 2b having already been tested in that role in May 1916 with bomb loads of 160 lbs.

   With the expansion of night bombing there was a shortfall in a medium point to point bomber. William Weir, the Air Minister, wanted an expansion of the bombing force to retaliate for the London air raids and to break the deadlock in the trenches. Production of the Beardmore powered F. E.2b was on the point of being phased out, but it was soon found it was the only suitable bomber for the role as envisaged by William Weir. Production re - commenced in March 1918, with contracts being placed with Garrett; Ransom, Sims & Jeffries and Weir at Cathcart, who sub - contracted their order to Stephens at Linthouse.

Weirs were fully stretched with the introduction of new types [the DH 9] and did not have the factory capacity to re - introduce production. Termed the "Night Flyer", the newly produced F. E.2bs were powered by the reliable 160 H.P. Beardmore. In service the undercarriage was modified to a simpler Vee structure, but basically the aeroplane was the same as it was when first produced in 1915. Other engines were installed in the airframe, but the mass - produced Beardmore was the most trusted and tried, giving the "Fee" a maximum speed of 91 M.P.H. Manufacture of the 160 H.P. engine reached a peak at Arrol -

Johnston during the five weeks of November 1917, with one hundred and sixty being produced. With the re - introduction of production of the F. E.2b, the firm of Crossley started to produce the 160 H.P. Beardmore in the spring of 1918, with production expected to end during December 1918.

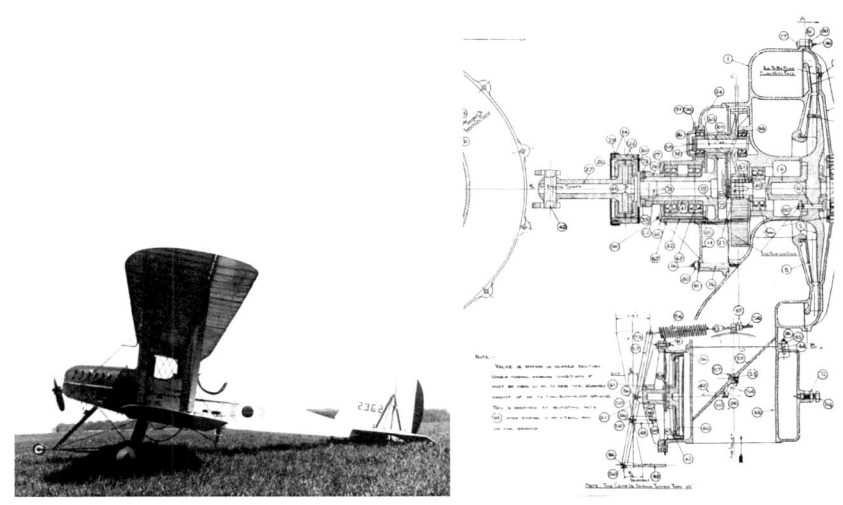

The R.E.7   The Beardmore test blower

The Armstrong Whitworth F.K.8   Norman Thompson school flying boat

The Central Aircraft Centaur

Lungwha Aircraft Factory, Schoettler design

As part of the Lord Weir/General Patrick agreement, 36 F.E.2bs were ordered for the United States Army Air Service (U.S.A.A.S). 32 were received by the Americans, three were retained by the British and one was wrecked in a crash before reaching Orly (E7075). 28 served with the 9th Aero Sqdn. U.S.A.A.S at Colombay - les - Belles, for duties with the British. The squadron was under the command of a British officer, Captain Smith.

As with most engines, the Beardmore power plant had its problems, mechanical and otherwise. Since it was based on German technology, most of the spares and auxiliaries came from that country. Most spares lasted into 1915 - 16 and they were frequently reconditioned for use. The Bosch oil pump was replaced during 1917 by the Murray Albion model which was much simpler and easier to make than the German type. Beardmore had produced their own carburettor for all the six cylinder models, but these were replaced by the Zenith 48 R.A. or the Brown and Barlow, which were again simpler to manufacture, since Beardmore could not guarantee delivery of their own carburettor model. In May 1917 during an examination by the Aeronautical Inspection Department, it was found that Arrol - Johnston had cast the engine block to the wrong specification, but by August 1917 the Ministry of Munitions had cleared up the problem. Another difficulty arose with the engines in France. Air mechanics noticed that the engines misfired and did not tick over at the specified speed when the engines were cold. When the spark plugs were inspected it was found that they were badly fouled and distorted. As with most in - line piston engines the worst spark plug was at number three cylinder. The pilots pointed out that the problem could be cured by running the engines faster. The makers then altered the hand book specification stating that the engine should be warmed at 1000 r.p.m. before flight. This simple instruction cured the difficulty. Another problem was investigated by the Royal Aircraft Factory in France, when it was found that the hold down bolts and cylinders had failed in service. The nuts had been incorrectly manufactured and they had become twisted when they were torqued against the washers, causing the studs to distort. One would stretch and the other bend, causing hammering. The Royal Aircraft Factory recommended that two flanges be cut in the block to give the nuts a good seating. This was done by the mechanics and the problem was cured. There were also problems with the water pump, oil filler caps and with the electrical system but, with time, these obstacles were overcome. The most pressing difficulty was with the engine magnetos and since they were German it was very difficult to replace them. Re - manufacture was tried but there were shortages of magnets, wire, and insulation tape and production capacity. The Admiralty supplied all magnetos from the British supplier until the Ministry of Munitions solved all the manufacturing problems and reduced the shortage.

On the 31st March 1918 there were two hundred and eight 120 H.P. Beardmore engines in service with two being written off and one thousand two hundred and eighty 160 H.P. Beardmores with 52 written off. The contractors, Arrol - Johnston and Crossley, had orders for 1050, which was cut to 750 at the end of April. The last order for Arrol - Johnston was for 23 engines to be made in December 1918. The final total of Beardmore aero - engines in wartime service was made on the 30th November 1918 when there were 1902, six cylinder models available.

After the Armistice it was expected that there would be a tremendous growth in air travel and the 160 H.P. Beardmore was to be used in many aeroplanes. The A. D. Channel was originally powered by the Hispano Suiza engine, but the first ten taken out of store had the 160 H.P. Beardmore fitted instead, with the first flying in June 1919. In 1920 four Channels were sold to Norway, but the engines were changed again to the 230 H.P. Siddeley Puma making them Channel IIs, with the same modification being carried out to one in Britain. This aeroplane, G - NZAI, was shipped out to New Zealand, surviving till 1945, when it was burned out in a fire. Another post -

war development was the Central aircraft Centaur 2A, which was designed by J. S. Fletcher. The first of its type, G - EAHR, was a twin engined, two bay biplane, flown at Martlesham Heath by Captain Courtney in July 1919. Unfortunately while it was coming into land at Northolt Aerodrome it crashed and was completely destroyed. The second production Centaur met the same fate at Northolt on 25th September 1920, when it too crashed after losing one engine.

The Avro 547 Triplane was built mainly from Avro 504 parts and it was to be powered by the 160 H.P. Beardmore, but little came in the way of orders for this aeroplane and it was dropped. Three Beardmore aero-engines found their way to China, where they were to be used in a Chinese aircraft factory. A local warlord had employed three German exiles to design aeroplanes for the factory, which was ten miles outside Shanghai. By 1923 the Lungwha Aircraft Factory was in operation, producing only two Beardmore powered aeroplanes, these aircraft flying until 1929. The arrival in China of more modern aeroplanes meant that production was curtailed, with the third Beardmore engine being used as spares. These were probably the last Beardmore powered aeroplanes to fly anywhere in the world.

(i)

Specifications
120 H.P.
Six cylinder water cooled, Lubrication pump capacity 3.5 pints, Crankcase capacity 4 pints.
Bore: 130 mm, **Stroke :** 175 mm, **Weight :** 420 lbs., **Power at 1200 r.p.m. =** 120 b. H.P.

160 H.P.
Six cylinder water cooled, Lubrication pump capacity 5 pints, Crankcase capacity 4 pints.
Bore: 142 mm, **Stroke:** 175 mm, **Weight:** 600 lbs., **Power at 1250 r.p.m.** = 166 b. H.P.

(ii)

Engines remaining on order
160 H.P. Beardmore
1 March 1917 = 650
1 March 1918 = 564

(iii)

Monthly deliveries of 160 H.P. Beardmore
From 1st January 1917

JAN	FEB	MAR	APR	MAY	JUN	JUL	AUG	SEP	OCT	NOV	DEC	JAN	FEB	MAR
30	40	76	31	55	76	65	58	87	112	160	142	139	135	104

(iv)

160 [120] H.P. Beardmore on Charge 31st March 1918

123 [17] **under repair**
465 **France**
 19 [11] **in service store**
118 **awaiting shipment to Egypt**
 91 **at contractors**
 23 [13] **Egypt 31. 1. 18**
 97 **at aircraft acceptance parks**
 7 [5] **Mesopotamia 31. 1. 18**
 10 **at mobilising squadrons**
 2 **Dover - Dunkirk**

205 [51] **training division**
1 [3] **training schools**
101 [80] **6th Brigade**
52 [2] **written off in March**
10 [16] **Sundry Units**
8 [7] **C. T. D.**
 1 **North West Frontier**   [NOTE: Four 120 H.P.'s obsolete]

(v)

American F.E.2b (Beardmore aero-engine)
Lord Weir/General Patrick agreement (ND)
Aircraft issued from Independent Air Force and British stocks flown to Orly from Lympne

D9227   D1873   D9115   D9765　C9802   A6460   D9908   D9910   D9916
D9912   B1877   A5650　A5671   A5692   D3751   D3521   E7075   E7068   E7072
E7076   D3785   D9915   E7095   E7100　E7102   E7090   E7106   E7110   D9959
D9942   B7923   D3782   C9821   D9969   D9970   D7099

(vi)

160 [120] H.P. Beardmore on Charge 30th November 1918

426 [12] **in transit for repair**
73 **6th Brigade**
41 [20] **in service store**
1 11th **[Irish Group]**
97 **at contractors**
14 [4] **sundry units**

114 **at aircraft acceptance works**
17 [2] **C. T. D.**
2 **S. E. Area**
503 **France**

129

36 [18] **S. W. Area**
26 **awaiting shipment to the East**
71 [15] **Midland Area**
109 [16] **Egypt and Palestine**
5 **N.E. Area**
73 **Salonika**

1 **N. W. Area**
11 [1] **Mesopotamia**
119 [29] **Schools**
3 **N. W. Frontier**
21 **Write offs in November**

(vii)

Estimated delivery of 160 H.P. Beardmore
21st March 1918

Contractor	Contract No.	Passed to Number	2 - 3 - 18	Apr	May	Jun	Jul	Aug
Arrol Johnston	34/A/21/c.21	200	22	30	40	50	48	-
Crossley	87. E. 230 AS.4/378/E	850	464	70	80	80	80	11
Total		1050	486	100	120	130	128	11

(viii)

Estimated delivery of 160 H.P. Beardmore
Powered aircraft
22nd April 1918

Contractor [F.E. 2b]	Contract No.	Passed to 30 - 3 -18 Number	May	June	July	Aug	Sep	Oct
Ransom Sims & Jeffries	AS29675 AS 2974	250	12	25	40	50	50	53
Weir [Stephens]	AS40317	150	3	20	25	25	25	25
Garrett	AS34281 65A/385/ C255	110	0	20	20	30	30	5

Contractor	Contract No.	Number	May	June	July	Aug	Sep	Oct
[A.W.F.K.8] Armstrong Whitworth Sanderson	AS13163 AS2829/18 AS3390	450	308	60	27			
	AS34715	200		32	65	43		

The B.H.P.

During 1915 and early 1916 the Airco company designed a large, two seat single engined aircraft around the 160 H.P. Beardmore. This aeroplane, the DH 4, was designed by Geoffrey de Havilland and is considered, today, to have been the best day bomber of the Great War. However shortages of the designated powerplant led to a rethink. When it was first flown at the Airco's works at Hendon in August 1916 by the designer, it was powered by an engine which was Beardmore in origin and to be the subject of much debate - the B.H.P.

The Aeronautical Inspection Directorate's inspector at Arrol - Johnston was Lieutenant Frank Halford and he is said to have persuaded T. C. Pullinger, the Managing Director, that the 160 H.P. Beardmore could be redesigned into a more powerful engine. Evidently his powers of persuasion were successful, for William Beardmore himself became involved in the new project, to be designated the "B.H.P." - "B" for Beardmore the financier, "H" for Halford the designer and "P" for Pullinger, who managed the scheme. This engine was to utilise much innovation in its design and construction. It was to use large amounts of aluminium in its cylinder block, which could be cast easily and be mass - produced in bulk. It also had aluminium pistons with rings of mild steel. It would appear that this engine had an ancestry going back to long before 1910. At that time T. C. Pullinger was Managing Director of New Arrol - Johnston at Paisley. One of their engineers, T. J. Biggs, designed an all-aluminium alloy engine with many of the features found today in the modern piston aero – engine, such as alloy block, inserted liners, overhead valves and camshaft. T. J. Biggs had been with Arrol - Johnston from 1902 and was involved in the production of the Arrol - Johnston Antarctic, a vehicle used by Shackleton in one of his Polar expeditions. This car had an alloy engine with three valves per cylinder, one inlet and two exhausts. In the same time scale Beardmore at Parkhead had developed an oil engine which had an overhead camshaft with overhead valves. Pullinger and William Beardmore therefore had the knowledge and experience of producing engines with the B.H.P. features, long before Frank Halford arrived at Heathfield and to back their involvement with these engines, both shared the patents for the detail design of the engine, including the valve arrangement.

Even with the B.H.P.'s now controversial background, the Beardmore company gave the credit for the design to T. J. Biggs, even though he had moved to Humber in 1912 and from there moved on to F. E. Baker in the autumn of 1914. At Bakers he designed a whole series of motor – cycles, including the Beardmore Precision, which was produced post - war. There is no other evidence to suggest in any of the surviving company records, contemporary magazines, books or otherwise, that Frank Halford contributed anything but his name to the B.H.P.

By the spring of 1915 it was evident that there would be a shortfall in the production of aero-engines. The War Office was employing twelve firms, including Arrol – Johnston at Heathfield, in the manufacture of engines. For high power aeroplane engines the British had to rely heavily on the French and it was not until the middle of 1916 that British high power aero - engines became available. One of these engines was the B.H.P. and in June 1916 its first bench trials were being run. This is the engine that was fitted to the D. H. 4 and in the autumn of 1916 it was sent to France for service trials.

To manufacture the new B.H.P. aero -engine Beardmore founded a new company, the Galloway Engineering Company, which was to have new works at Tongland in Kirkcudbrightshire. Due to its design and construction it was felt by the Director of Military Aeronautics that the B.H.P. would be ideal to mass produce. However there was a problem. By the end of December 1916 twenty six firms were involved in aero - engine production and there was no clear cut policy for production, from either the War Office or the Admiralty.
There was still a shortage of engines, particularly the B.H.P., so by the end of the year there was complete confusion on engine supply.

In January 1917, American born Percy Martin, formerly managing director of the Daimler Company and B.S.A., took over as Controller for Petrol Engines at the Ministry of Munitions. He was to allocate engines to all the different departments and by the summer he ratified the designs and concentrated production on thirteen types. The reason for this was quite clear, there were too many aero - engines in production, some were not so good, while others, like the Rolls -

Royce Falcon were very popular with the pilots. Resources and production time were very limited and William Weir, Director General of Aircraft Production at the Ministry of Munitions, recognised this and embarked on an engine production programme. As the minister responsible for aircraft production, Weir felt that the B.H.P. was the best engine for mass production. Weir had a vested interest in the B.H.P. His company, J. & G. Weir, had been selected as a sub - contractor to supply the aluminium cylinder blocks for the major manufacturer the Siddeley - Deasy Company. Sometime earlier this firm had become involved in the discussion of how the engine was to be made. On Saturday 7th October 1916, at the Station Hotel, Dumfries, the interested parties in the B.H.P. engine programme had met. They were: Latta and Lang from Weirs, Pullinger from Arrol - Johnston, Bagnall - Wilde from the War Office, Halford in uniform and Mr Siddeley. By that time two, B.H.P. aero - engines had been made by the Galloway Engineering Company; one had completed sixteen hours bench tests while the other had been installed in the prototype D.H. 4. At the meeting all discussed the potential of the engine and its production problems and difficulties. John Siddeley said he could produce fifty engines a week, even though he had a full order book, while Pullinger declared that if his firm had the parts they could produce fifteen engines a week. Bagnall - Wilde said it looked like a good engine because it could be run for eighty hours between overhauls. The Station Hotel meeting was very important, because it was to set the pattern of supply through sub - contracts for the major manufacturers, Galloway Engineering and the Siddeley- Deasy Company. Weirs promised that they could produce one hundred and thirty machined cylinder blocks per week and three hundred and ninety cylinder liners, but the problem for Weirs was the availability of skilled labour. The cylinder liners were to be manufactured by women workers whose only skill had been in producing shell cases. Weirs had the equipment for boring out the cylinder blocks, but they pressed Bagnall - Wilde of the War Office for a grant to obtain more plant. After the meeting Pullinger allowed Latta and Lang to take away a cylinder block and three liners to make a pattern for the engine. Weirs were then to try a production run to see if they had the space and the capacity to do the job.

T.J. Biggs　　　　T. C. Pullinger　　　　Frank Halford

Galloway 200 H.P. B.H.P.　　　　Siddeley 200 H.P. B.H.P

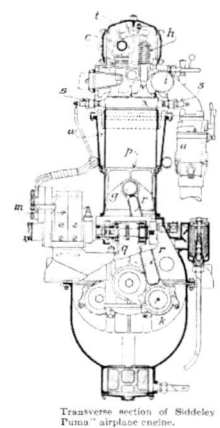 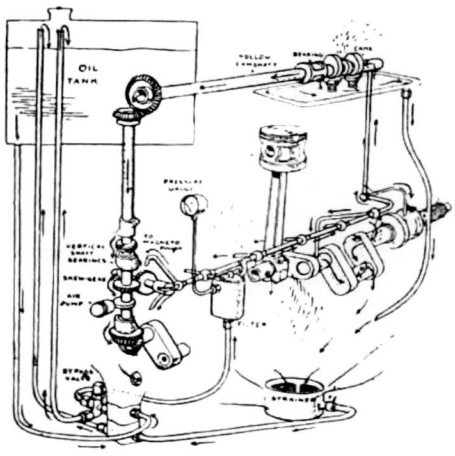

Profile of the Siddeley Puma　　　Oil circulation of B.H.P./Puma

It was also becoming increasingly clear that, with the production targets being discussed, Galloway Engineering did not have the facilities to undertake mass production. By now John Siddeley had become non-committal, but his presence was necessary to find out if his company could agree to take on production of the engine. When he was questioned about the display engine he said nothing.

    The main problem, and maybe John Siddeley recognised this, was that the first two engines had had all their faults eliminated; the engine had never been tried and tested with a full production batch. During production the B.H.P. developed marked defects in the manufacturing process. It could be made quite easily at Galloway Engineering, where there was a small production team, but with Siddeley Deasy it was a different story. In order to obtain bulk production, John Siddeley had altered the design radically apparently without telling the Ministry of Munitions or the War Office. Since the B.H.P. was protected by joint Beardmore - Pullinger patents, the John Siddeley redesign was in all probability to by - pass royalties on patents. The initial design of the B.H.P. engine was wholly original. The mass production of the cylinder blocks now required a large amount of development time and delayed the programme by six months. The new crankshaft was subject to delay because the sub - contractors did not have the skill or the manufacturing capacity. In June 1917 crankshaft orders had to be placed in America and with that came the problem of supplying drawings, sending prints and drawing up contracts. This resulted in a delay of four months, but by October supplies of crankshafts started to arrive from America and the position became more satisfactory. By then William Weir was writing, "The B.H.P. is getting better and better," and now he had the support of Percy Martin, who backed Weir's judgment by selecting the B.H.P. for the 1917 - 18 aero - engine programme. It was to be in the 200 H.P. class with the others being the Hispano - Suiza, B.R. 2, Sunbeam Arab and the American produced Liberty. Though it was ordered as early as December 1916 the B.H.P. wasn't even ready for bulk production in September 1917, when the programme was to be in its stride. It was found that the oldest engines were the best, since they had been under test for so long that all their troubles had been eliminated. Interchangeability of engines with airframes was the key to the aero-engine programme but on the D.H. 4, powered by the Rolls - Royce Eagle, it just did not work. It was found that the Rolls - Royce engine cowlings matched the airframe, but when fitted with the Siddeley B.H.P., they did not mate up. This meant that the D.H. 4 fitted with the Siddeley B.H.P. had to have an extensive redesign. During June and July 1917 seven test aircraft were allocated for the B.H.P. programme including one obsolete. The new D.H 9 flew with a Galloway B.H.P. at the test squadron and they found its performance was superior to the Eagle engined D.H. 4. With the D.H. 4 there was also a propeller test with three being tried to find the most efficient. By now fifty cylinder blocks were being made per week.

However there were more problems with the ignition system and the magneto. By 12th June 1917 Major Meade of the Controller Technical Department submitted a report stating that the troubles associated with the B.H.P. programme were normal for this type of engine, "Lack of attention to detail and the quality of workmanship" was the problem he wrote. As the designated bomber engine for the D.H. 4 and D.H 9 with others, under test the engines failed to develop their full power. This lack of power was found to be caused by bad tuning at the factory. The Royal Aircraft Factory then had to investigate the Siddeley production methods and also compression and supercharging of selected engines. In June 1917 Weirs sent Siddeley Deasy two cylinder blocks made of an alloy of copper, zinc and tin to be made up into a new engine. This engine was the first wholly Siddeley built B.H.P. Their first one, though, used a Galloway crankshaft, con - rods and overhead camshaft in its construction and had blocks made of copper and tin. The new Weir cylinder blocks

D. H. 4 with the Galloway B.H.P.

The D.H. 9

D.H. 9 ready for delivery at Renfrew

Weir assembled D.H. 9s in Glasgow

Members of the 148th Aero Squadron on a D.H.9 daylight raid, August 5th 1918, R.A.F. Pilot Maj. Hales, film Cameraman Cpl. Schneider and Lieut. E.O. Harrs in coat.

Puma engined Bristol Fighter

The ungainly Sopwith Rhino

The Bristol Braemar   A 200 H.P. B.H.P. in 1918

A post – war Bristol 47 Tourer powered by an Armstrong Siddeley Puma, owned by S. Instone and Co., Ltd Flew from 1920 to February 1921

were thirty nine pounds lighter than the originals and the whole engine was ready for running on Thursday 5th June 1917. It was tested for one hundred and sixteen hours at 1400 R.P.M. developing 215 H.P. After this test it was found that the valves were badly worn with premature wear on their seating. This was an indication of what was to follow when the engines were put into service. When climbing to altitude steam formed in the rear cylinders of the D.H 4 and the engines overheated. This fault was cured by copying the German system which was found in the Aviatik powered by the 230 H.P. Benz. A branch pipe was taken from the top of the rear cylinders and fed into the carburettor jacket. The B.H.P. was also tested at Hendon with a supercharger during the same test period and after reprofiling the camshaft the engine showed a considerable improvement on performance. By August 1917 the B.H.P.'s compression ratio was raised. Two types were tried, 5.2: 1 and 5.1: 1 with a D. H. 4 [A7671] being used to test the spark plugs and their seating.

As a private venture, Sopwith received a licence to build a prototype around the B.H.P. This was the Sopwith Rhino. It never came up to expectation, because, when tested against the similarly powered D.H 9 it was considerably slower. At ten thousand feet, with the same military bomb load, it could barely keep up with the D.H 9. One Bristol fighter [B1206] when flown with the B.H.P., was found to have a similar performance to the Rolls - Royce Falcon. This anomaly was caused by the same problem which was to recur time and time again; the oldest engines had all their faults eradicated. The first Siddeley built engines were tested in the D.H 9, C6053, over a two hundred hour period with a full military load, in flights of eight hours and five and a half hours endurance. With these flights came technical problems. Faulty lubrication caused bearing failure, back firing in the carburettor [cured by fitting new intake pipes] cutting out and one con - rod failure. On the whole at, Martlesham Heath, the B.H.P. powered aeroplanes were found to be running well apart from the minor problems mentioned above.

The D.H. 4 had started military operations in France as early as March 1917 and the D.H 9 was intended as its long range replacement. The wings and tail of the D.H. 4 were identical to the D.H 9, but in the Four the fuel tank separated the crew. In the Nine the pilot sat behind the fuel tank and had better communication with the air gunner. They were literally in touch with each other. Its fighting qualities were felt to be superior to the D.H. 4. On many occasions formations of D.H 9 were able to outfight their attackers, whereas the earlier aeroplane would have been slaughtered. For photographic reconnaissance the D.H 9 flew at an altitude of ten thousand feet to obtain the correct overlay patch work for the photographic interpreters and map makers. At this altitude German anti - aircraft fire was accurate and deadly, resulting in heavy losses.

Many of the orders for D.H.4 were changed to D.H 9 at the express wish of William Weir. He wanted to create a surplus of airframes and he felt that the D.H 9 was ideal for mass production. He was backed by General Pitcher and the designer of the aeroplane, Geoffrey de Havilland. As a result of the Germans bombing London a further total of one thousand for the D.H 9 were authorised on 24th October 1917, all to be powered by the Galloway/Siddeley Deasy B.H.P.

At the end of March 1918 it was decided to name all the aero-engines and rename types already in service. The Galloway B.H.P. was typed as the 200 H.P. B.H.P.G. 2, while the Siddeley B.H.P. was designated as the 200 H.P. B.H.P.S. 1. The Galloway B.H.P. became the Galloway Adriatic, while the Siddeley Deasy B.H.P. became the Siddeley Puma. Galloway Engineering never had the capacity to produce the B.H.P. in quantity, only building about a hundred of the type, but it was felt by the Ministry of Munitions that it was better to produce than say, a Rolls - Royce. Though it was supposed to be an all alloy engine the first ten Galloway B.H.P.s ran with cast iron cylinder heads. Siddeley Deasy's methods of production meant that initially the engines were basically the same, but once they were mass produced there were many differences, including the compression ratio. Both engines had not yet reached the peak of their development, but, when they reached the air services performance, particularly that of the Siddeley Deasy B.H.P. was way below what was specified. With the Armistice came the eventual cancellation and settlements of contracts. In its Puma form the B.H.P. went on to become one of the finest six cylinder aero - engines ever built, powering many record breaking aeroplanes. When they were pressed into military service many B.H.Ps never produced the required power and gained a bad performance reputation with some aircrews. With Trenchard's Independent Air Force, the B.H.P. powered aeroplanes were used aggressively, but this was due to the tenacity of the crews than the powerplant. It was always a bone of contention between William Weir, now the Air Minister and Hugh Trenchard, that the B.H.P. never lived up to its early expectations.

Some of the more learned authorities describe the B.H.P. powered D.H 9 as a failure. However a contemporary American report fully praised the D.H 9 against its stablemate the D.H. 4, "The D.H.9 type is unquestionably much superior and our failure to provide them resulted in serious damage to morale." The report declared. During the post - war years the design reached its zenith with the Liberty powered D.H 9a or Ninaak, its superb reputation being won over the battlefields of France in 1917 - 18.

Even in peace, controversy still followed the B.H.P. The Siddeley - Deasy Company refused to honour its war break contracts with one of the Glasgow suppliers of cylinder liners – Weir. James Latta of Weir also put in a claim to the Royal Commission on Awards to Inventors for a payment on the strength of a valve design for the B.H.P engine. This claim was rejected, but when Frank Halford was questioned by the Commission about the time scale of the design and his involvement with the project, he suffered a lapse of memory and could not recall any of the dates or details of the engine to the Commission. This put him into conflict with William Beardmore and T. C. Pullinger who cornered him on the steps of the Commission building, asking him what he was up to. (Witnessed by a Glasgow Herald reporter.) Both Pullinger and Beardmore emphasised the extent of their influence on the design, but the Royal Commission paid out £20000 to Beardmore, Halford and Pullinger, making the award a three way split for their contribution to the war effort. In some way Halford gets all the credit for the B.H.P. design and T.J. Biggs is quietly forgotten.

(i)

B.H.P

Bore: 145 mm **Stroke:** 190 mm **Maximum Break Horse Power:** 256
Weight: 645 lbs. **Normal R.P.M.:** 1400 **Max:** 1500
Note: Six cylinder, water cooled in - line with three valves per cylinder, one inlet two exhaust.

(ii)

B.H.P. Engines on order
1st March each year

1917	3000
1918	453

(iii)

B.H.P. Deliveries from Jan. 1917 to 31st March 1918

Jan	Feb	Mar	Apl	May	Jun	Jul	Aug	Sept	Oct	Nov	Dec	Jan	Feb	Mar
0	0	0	2	2	2	7	18	45	45	52	144	256	255	258

(iv)

B.H.P. ENGINES on charge 31st March 1918

Galloway B.H.P   72 [One write off]
Siddeley Deasy B.H.P   1078 [Nine write offs]

(v)

Estimated delivery of B.H.P. aero - engines 22nd April 1918

Passed

Contractor	Contract Number	30 Mar	May	Jun	Jul	Aug	Sep	Oct	Nov
Beardmore	AS 27579	40	8	10	10	2			
Siddeley Deasy	87E649 AS1874/18/E	5000	1048	400	500	550	550	550	552

(**Note**: Notice how in this case the contractor is Beardmore and not Galloway Engineering)

(vi)

Contractors for B.H.P powered DH 9 22nd April 1918

Contractor	Contract	Order	Passed to 30. 3. 18
Berwick	87A1185 AS3772	110	7
Crossley	AS32754	500	2
Cubitt	AS26928	800	1
Vulcan	35A/414/C293	100	0
Westland	35A/415/C295	150	67
Mann Eggerton	35A/413/C292	100	11
Weir	AS17570	400	32
Waring & Gillow	35A/416/C295	500	36
Short	AS34886	100	25
Whitehead	AS2341/18	100	0
Airco	AS 17569	900	0

FIELD IMPROVEMENTS ON THE D.H 9

Alteration of Zenith Carburettor

Of the experiments conducted by the R.A.F. squadrons the most important is the alteration on the Zenith carburettor which enables the D. H. 9 machine with the 240 B.H.P. engine to climb from four to six thousand feet higher than formerly. This alteration concerns the device which regulates the proportion of petrol and air at high altitudes. As the density of air, consequently the amount of oxygen decreases at high altitudes and makes the mixture too rich, a carburettor adjustment must either supply more air or decrease the petrol supply in order to maintain a properly proportioned combustible mixture. The altitude adjustment on the Zenith carburettor cuts down the supply of petrol by opening a by-pass from the mixing tube to the float-chamber which tends to lessen the difference in air pressure on the petrol. Since the suction is decreased the flow of petrol diminishes correspondingly. The Improvement on this adjustment is an increase in the size of the bypass and the use of larger choke (Venturi) tube. It is claimed that the average B.H.P. engine fitted with Zenith carburettors altered in this way, will take the D. H. 9 up to eighteen thousand feet.

Stabilizer Brace

An addition to the rigging of the D.H 9 is a small, streamlined brace from the fuselage to the front spar of the horizontal stabilizer. This brace keeps the spar straight and prevents warping or collapsing of the stabilizer but of course adds to the "head-resistance."

Magneto Door

A larger door in the fuselage side, opposite the magneto, makes it easier for the engine mechanic to check the "break" in the interrupter-points and also makes a general inspection of the magnetos possible without the removal of the upper engine cowlings.

Long Exhaust Pipes

By replacing the two short exhaust outlet pipes from the exhaust-manifold, with four longer pipes, engine back-pressure is slightly relieved and the exhaust gases and soot are kept from blowing in to the faces of the pilot and observer.

(B.E.F. American Liaison Officer June 1918)

THE EAGLE INSURANCE

By January 1918 the supply of aero - engines from Rolls - Royce was causing great concern to the air services. Rolls - Royce engines were very labour intensive, they required a lot of machine tooling during their production and they were also using a great deal of materials which were then in short supply. The Ministry of Munitions decided to post into Rolls – Royce Sir A. Herbert, with his own supply branch from the department. Great changes had also come about with a difference in aircraft policy and engine procurement. The Rolls - Royce Eagle VIII had been chosen, much against the wishes of the Ministry of Munitions, as the engine for the new bomber programme, particularly for the V/1500. The projected output of this engine was two hundred per week, but on the 22nd April 1918 an order for two hundred Galloway Atlantics was recorded as an insurance against failure of Rolls - Royce supplying the Eagles.

The Galloway Atlantic was built up from two B.H.P. cylinder blocks bolted as a V on to a common crankcase. Though it shared some of the B.H.P.'s deficiencies, such as burnt out valves and leaking cylinder heads, development proceeded. A prototype Atlantic was fitted to a D.H 9 and by the 31st May 1918 four were ready for installation in aircraft. The Siddeley concern took a part in this engine's development when they fitted their own B.H.P. cylinder blocks to the same crankcase and called the engine the Atlantic Puma [Pacific] making this engine identical to the Galloway Atlantic. Latterly the Atlantic Puma [Pacific] became the Siddeley Pacific.

The introduction of the Rolls - Royce Eagle VIII aero - engine for the V/1500 bomber programme was very slow and Rolls - Royce were able to keep pace with the aeroplane's production. Consequently at an Air Board meeting on 30th July 1918 the order for two hundred Galloway Atlantics was allowed to stand, but there were to be no re - orders. By 30th November 1918 Galloway and Siddeley Deasy had produced thirty Galloway Atlantics with four having been fitted to the Beardmore V/1500 in August/September. These engines were at Galloway/Siddeley Deasy [6], at a training school [1], with the C.T.D [8], Midlands [2], in service store [1],under repair [12]. For Siddeley Deasy they perfected the B.H.P. in its Puma form and followed the Atlantic design further by manufacturing the Tiger engine using production Puma cylinder blocks. The Siddeley Tiger engine was fitted into the Siddeley Sinai heavy gun bomber of the post war period, but it was not a success. The same could be said for the Galloway Atlantic. Beardmore were to fit the powerplant to the W.B. VIa and the W.B. VIII, but sadly the combination came to nothing.

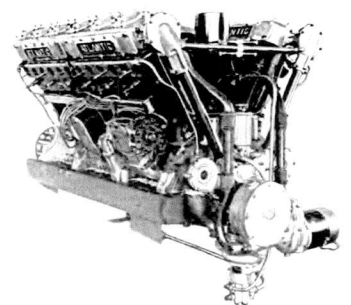

The Galloway Atlantic

200 H.P Galloway Adriatic   The Rolls Royce Eagle

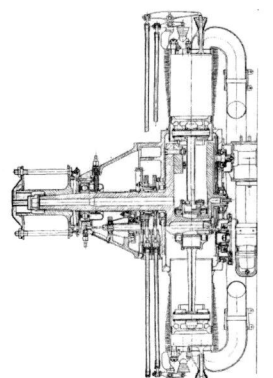 

The A.B.C. Dragonfly to be produced at Crossmyloof Ice Rink

The Armstrong Siddeley Tiger produced with Puma cylinder blocks

The Armstrong Siddeley Sinai

The Air Board decision of 30th July effectively meant the end of the Austro - Daimler series of aero-engines and the B.H.P. for the Beardmore Group, Arrol Johnston and Galloway Engineering. As part of the rationalisation of the power plants for the 1918 aero - engine programme the Air Board had selected the A.B.C. Dragonfly as one of its most promising designs. The Dragonfly came in two types, seven cylinder and a nine cylinder models. They were all designed by Granville Bradshaw of Walton Motors. The Beardmore Group were tasked to build the nine cylinder Dragonfly 1a, probably for installation in Barclay Curle built fighters or other designs. A direct competitor to the Dragonfly engine was W.O. Bentley's B.R. 2 and both these engines were expected to replace a whole range of power plants between 1st July 1918 and 30th June 1919, a staggering total of 15970 aero - engines. As an advance for production Beardmore received £100000 from the Ministry of Munitions. The Air Board decision had been preceded on 8th June 1918 when Beardmore received an order for 1000 A.B.C. Dragonfly II engines to contract 34a/651/C58. Later this order was increased by five hundred. To produce this engine, Beardmore bought the Crossmyloof Ice Rink on Glasgow's south side for £17000. One of the reasons the Dragonfly was ordered was that it did not require much in the way of skilled labour and most of the shell manufacturing machinery could be used to turn out the engine cylinders. It was then found that the performance of the A.B.C. Dragonfly was not up to expectations and it was regarded as a failure. Even into the nineteen twenties the Royal Aircraft Establishment tried to cure the Dragonfly's problems, but without success. At one of its director meetings the board of William Beardmore & Co., Ltd. was informed that that the Dragonfly programme was cancelled as of 13th May 1919. No Dragonfly aero - engines were made at Crossmyloof, except for a batch of crankshafts, leaving the company to use the premises as a store.

As a means of diversification in 1920, Galloway Engineering went on to produce motor cars for its subsidiary Galloway Motors. William Beardmore hoped that Galloway Engineering would produce aero – engines, such as the Adriatic, for his company's aircraft designs, but by 1920 no orders had materialised. By 1926 the Aircraft Disposal Company were selling off Galloway Atlantics to anyone. Some were bought by American smugglers and fitted to high speed launches during America's prohibition era, showing the American Customs a clean pair of heels. Due to the prevailing economic conditions at the time, William Beardmore liquidated Galloway Engineering and its subsidiary Galloway Motors in 1928. These companies were never part of the William Beardmore & Co., Ltd. organisation, but a part of his own private interests.

(i)

Galloway Atlantic
Bore: 145 mm   **Stroke:** 190 mm   **Max. B.H.P.:** 575
Weight: 1145 lbs. **Normal R.P.M.:** 1500 **Maximum R.P.M.:** 1600
Note: Twelve cylinder liquid cooled with two rows of six cylinders set at an angle of 90º.

(ii)

Beardmore built ABC Dragonfly
Bore: 140 mm   **Stroke:** 165 mm **Max B.H.P.:** 350   **Max. R.P.M.:** 1750
Compression Ratio: 4.025: 1 **Note:** Nine cylinder air cooled radial with three valves per cylinder of two exhaust and one inlet.

The Sopwith Dragon and the Austin Greyhound with the A.B.C. Dragonfly

AERO - ENGINES POST WAR

After the Armistice the company continued to develop aero - engines and as a means of consolidation bought the entire stock of old Arrol Johnston built Austro – Daimlers from the Air Ministry. To increase the power of the engine the cylinders were once more bored out, bringing the horse power up to180 H.P. One example of this type was sold to F. E. Baker who ran it on gas at their Birmingham works.

Unfortunately for Beardmore a new firm had been set up to sell off all the surplus engines and aeroplanes from the Great War. This was the Aircraft Disposal Company [A. D. C.] Clearly the old Austro - Daimler series was obsolete and Beardmore were to pay a high price for their initial enthusiasm. The A. D. C. started to sell off its vast store of modern engines at scrap prices and no - one displayed any interest in buying in bulk the vast stock of 120 H.P./160 H.P. and 180 H.P. Beardmore aero – engines from William Beardmore & Co. Ltd. The A. D. C. went further and started to sell versions of the D.H 9 with the Rolls - Royce Eagle engine calling it the D.H. 9b. Beardmore then decided to stop selling their old series of engines and concentrate now on building newer models.

The Beardmore works at Coatbridge was to be the centre of production for this new series of engines. Earlier, Coatbridge had built an experimental aero - engine in 1917, but little detail of this engine exists. From the Ministry of Munitions Beardmore brought in Alan Chorlton, who had been Deputy Director of Petrol Engines under Percy Martin. Before the war Chorlton had been the chief engineer of Ruston, Hornsby & Co., a firm which had developed a series of stationary oil engines for power houses. Alan Chorlton is credited with developing a compromise rotary engine and was a trustee of the Italian Tossi engine. He joined William Beardmore & Co. Ltd. during May 1918 and by 1919 had commenced on further experimental work at Coatbridge. With the failure of the post - war plan for aero - engine production Beardmore transferred their operation to "M" shop at Parkhead.

Although the experimental work had started with aero - engines as early as 1917 the new series of aero - engines had little in common with anything Beardmore had done before. Engines in those days worked at very low compressions due to the quality of the fuel and by October 1920 Alan Chorlton felt that these low compressions, especially found in the crude oil - engine, would be an ideal powerplant for airships. These new engines were called compression ignition types or as we call them today, diesels. Early in 1921 Harry Ricardo, the government's advisor on aero - engines, published a paper on low compression engines that could burn cheap fuels and he proposed that these engines be used in aeroplanes. By 1922 a six cylinder aero - engine of 700 H.P. was at test in the engine shed at Rigby Street, Parkhead. This engine was the Beardmore Cyclone Mk 1 of 8 5/8ths bore, with a stroke of twelve inches, to be fuelled by petrol. The crankshaft was at the top with the cylinder head at the bottom, with four valves per cylinder. Beardmore advertised this engine as the inverted water cooled Cyclone Mk1 which could be fitted to rail cars as well as aeroplanes. By 1926 the Cyclone Mk 1 became the Cyclone Mk II with a much more conventional layout, with the cylinder head at the top. It had exactly the same dimensions as the earlier engine with a weight of two 2155 lbs. producing over 900 H.P. at 1350 r.p.m. This engine had no propeller reduction gearing, the airscrew being bolted straight on to the crankshaft flange. Tests were carried out on this engine at Parkhead, with only one being recorded as built, this being sold to the German aircraft manufacturer Ernst Heinkel.

The next engine developed at Parkhead to the designs of Alan Chorlton was the Beardmore Typhoon. It shared many of the design features of the Cyclone, such as the same bore and stroke, but this engine was a compression ignition type, fuelled by oil. It was a water cooled engine and produced 800 H.P. at over 1000 r.p.m. This engine was first used by Canadian National Railways in their rail cars during the mid-twenties and was regarded by them as a success. A petrol version of this engine was also made, called the Typhoon II and it shared many of the features of the Typhoon I. The six cylinder layout had been chosen by Beardmore for its economy and reliability. By using inversion they felt the thrust line would be kept in its natural position, make less noise, offer a narrower obstruction to the pilot and give better gravity feed for the fuel. Production would also be far simpler because there were fewer working parts in the engine, the cylinder covers could be removed, valve gear dismantled for regrinding and the con. rods and pistons could be removed without dismantling the whole engine.

At the end of 1926 the Beardmore Typhoon II was fitted to an Avro Aldershot [J6852] and on Monday 24th January 1927 the Typhoon II finally took to the air. The Typhoon required no mechanical starter which other contemporary engines used and in this case a gas starter was fitted. No difficulties were encountered on start up, but at idling speed it occasionally misfired, causing the engine to flick visibly at the cylinder head. Each cylinder developed 150 H.P., with a fuel consumption which was much less than that of a similar six cylinder engine. On the Aldershot the Beardmore Typhoon required no special fittings even though the aircraft had been designed for the much bigger Napier Lion. The engine was mounted on four steel tubes which were attached to the Typhoon crankcase; two ran to the bottom of the fuselage, while the other two ran to the centre - section of the airframe. When Bert Hinkler opened the throttle the Aldershot took off in a remarkably short run and in the air it ran smoothly. The Typhoon gave the pilot a better view from the cockpit than when it was powered with the Napier Lion and in the air Hinkler appeared to be pleased with the Aldershot/Typhoon combination showing the spectators aerobatics before landing. To produce more power from the same basic design, the Cyclone/Typhoon crankshaft was lengthened and two more cylinders were added making it an eight cylinder model. As the Beardmore Simoon, it had a bore of nearly nine inches, but the stroke remained the same at twelve inches. The cylinder crankcase was of aluminium, with steel liners and each cylinder had its own

The Beardmore Typhoon

The Beardmore Cyclone Mk1

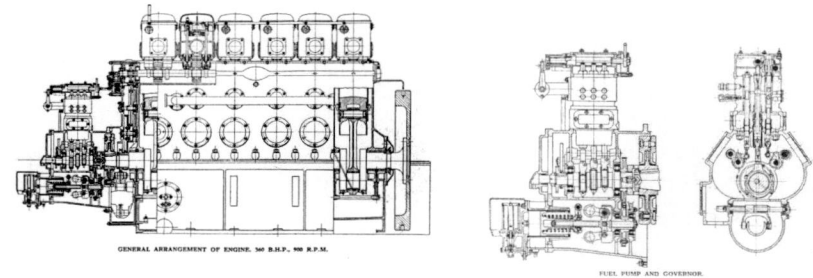

The six cylinder compression ignition Hurricane engine

The original Avro Aldershot   The Typhoon/Aldershot combination

The Beardmore Simoon flew in the Blackburn Cubaroo N167

 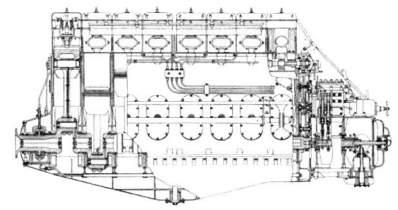

The Beardmore Tornado 8 cylinder compression ignition engine, later mark

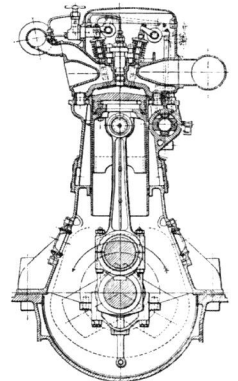 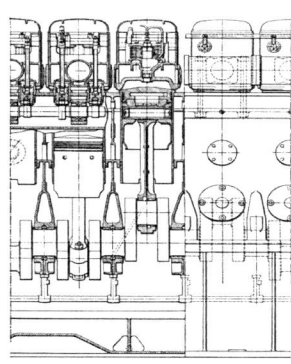

Profiles of the early Tornado

separate head casting which was attached to the block by the valve gear. One Simoon was fitted to a Blackburn Cubaroo [N167] during 1926. There are few accounts of this engine in the Cubaroo, except to say that it was powered by a petrol engine.

Earlier in 1923 the Air Ministry began to take an active interest in these Parkhead aero - engines. The Air Minister, Samuel Hoare, confirmed to Parliament that the Air Ministry was taking an active interest in producing a compression ignition engine for aircraft use. Then in 1924 Beardmore received a contract to supply nine Typhoon aero - engines to the Air Ministry, to contracts A.M. 438600/23 and A.M. 433735/23. This work lasted into 1925 and was priced through Beardmore's accounts at £8820: 11s: 7d, but to the Air Ministry it was considerably more, £21968, with one payment being for £15112. The costing of these engines was the subject of a Treasury enquiry resulting in Air Commodore Dowding receiving much negative correspondence from the Treasury.

The Air Ministry had chosen these engines for the new airship programme which was to be launched for Empire development during the late nineteen twenties. The airship programme centred around two airships the R100 and the R101. The R100 was to be manufactured by a subsidiary of Vickers, the Airship Guarantee Company, while the R101 was to be built by the Air Ministry at its Cardington works. The Beardmore engines had been chosen because they did not use petrol. There was a limited fire risk because there was no ignition system which could cause sparks and set the airship gas, hydrogen, on fire. It was also felt that in the hot Empire routes petrol would turn bad, be difficult to store and evaporate quickly. Vickers also selected the Typhoon for their airship and during July 1926 they approached the company for quotes and specifications. These negotiations came to nothing and Vickers went on to select second - hand Rolls - Royce petrol aero - engines for the R100. During late 1926 the Air Ministry changed its requirements for airship engines when it ordered a new Beardmore engine from Parkhead. The Air Ministry felt that the Typhoon had reached the end of its development life and a newer engine needed to be substituted. During discussions with Beardmore the six cylinder engine was referred to as the Beardmore Hurricane, but in fact it was the same basic Typhoon model. What Alan Chorlton developed was an eight cylinder compression ignition aero - engine, a more violent Hurricane - the Beardmore Tornado. The Air Ministry now ordered six Tornadoes and one spare to contract A.M. 937947. The Beardmore Tornado was now to be linked closely to the development of the government's airship, the R101.

The Tornado was produced from the Cyclone/Typhoon series and was an ultimate development of the Beardmore Simoon. Before it was fitted to the R101 it went through three separate design phases with regard to cylinder block, crankshafts, oil injectors and inspection covers, with the initial block casting being completed by Clyde Alloy. The Tornado was an eight cylinder in - line with a bore of 8 1/4" and a stroke of twelve inches, producing 650 H.P. at 1000 r.p.m. Each cylinder had four valves, two inlet and two exhaust, making the Beardmore Tornado a semi - diesel. The crankcase was of monobloc construction and was cast in two types, one of steel weighing 4600 lbs. while the other was of aluminium weighing 3600 lbs. All of the design detail was left to Alan Chorlton, such as the fitting of four oil pumps which fed the eight cylinders with a constant supply of oil at a fixed pressure. A switch valve was connected between the pumps which were at the front of the engine and ensured the correct timing of each fuel injection to the two cylinders and their atomisers. Fuel injection took place just before top dead centre, but there was a problem; the atomisers choked because of the fuel quality and Chorlton had to design a miniature filter for each atomiser to stop the jets from blocking. Alan Chorlton also fitted an anti - backfire device to each engine which worked under test at Parkhead.

On the R101 the two hundred and forty gallon fuel tanks were grouped near the passenger compartment, which was sufficient for each engine to run for eight hours at full power. In the event of an accident these tanks could be emptied in eleven seconds and when they were tested for the first time the tanks collapsed due to pressure changes caused by the size of the breather hole. Fuel for the Tornado engines was either Shell - Mex or Anglo - Persian. In the R101 the fuel pipes in the hull were fifteen hundred feet in length, while the water pipes were nearly six hundred feet. The Beardmore Tornado was fitted into special engine pods which had been designed by Commander Cave - Brown - Cave to give the minimum of drag on the airship. This ensured easy servicing for the engines during flight and they could be removed quickly and easily on the ground. The Tornado was also provided with three triangular radiators mounted above the engine pod, which provided steam cooling. The Tornado engine pods were situated on either side of frame four, higher up on both sides of frame nine and centrally under frame eleven.

For starting, the five Tornado engines' five auxiliary 40 H.P. motors were installed in rails in the power pods. These small engines also drove three electrical generators and two air compressors and were cooled with water from the main engines. The main weakness of these starter motors was that they were fuelled with petrol, but to get round this hazard the petrol supply was delivered from fuel tanks that could be dropped from the airship in the event of fire. To help the airship manoeuvre as it docked the propellers were designed to rotate around their hubs giving ahead or astern thrust or be retained in their neutral position. When tested initially at the gantry in Parkhead the whole propeller system worked well. The first propellers tested were of hollow steel and it was found that they worked well, but when fitted to the Tornado and run at full speed they broke up. Solid alloy propellers were tried, which were fitted to the same hubs as the hollow airscrews. The hubs were modified to take the greater centrifugal force of the heavier blade. As an insurance against the failure of the metal blades Commander Cave - Brown - Cave suggested that wooden propeller blades be used instead, with one being used for astern thrust. These blades had a diameter of sixteen feet.

Other tests were carried out and the engine oil system was investigated. A unique system of utilising the inside of the engine for oil cooling was tried. Air was drawn into the crankcase to act as a heat exchanger, but this led to a failure of the oil system and the trial engine based on four Beardmore Tornado cylinders burnt out. It was also discovered that the fine mixture of oil spray and air was highly explosive and the whole idea was dropped. The Tornado went back to conventional oil coolers.

While the Beardmore Tornado was being produced and developed, three other oil engines were being tested abroad. In Germany the Junkers concern was developing a double six engine of 600 H.P. Napier received a licence to build them in this country as the Napier Culvern and three were fitted to a flying boat for an Air Ministry trial. Another Culvern was installed by Hawkers into a Horsley air frame for further experiments. In this country Rolls - Royce developed an oil engine from the Condor, but it was a failure. In America, Packard fitted a nine cylinder radial air cooled oil engine into an aircraft, but it was not a success. Only the Junkers concern made any headway, fitting the engine into examples of its aircraft such as the J.U.52 and J.U.86 and some Dornier flying boats. Russia took an interest in these engines, but little detail exists on their development.

Most of the initial engine trials were carried out at Parkhead and at the Royal Aircraft Establishment at Farnborough. The engine installation on R101 was reported as being completed on 24th September 1930. She was scheduled for her proving flight to Karachi in the autumn of 1930 with the Air Minister Lord Thomson and a large entourage, but it was felt in some quarters that the Tornadoes had not been tried and tested properly. The first Tornado is reported as being delivered on 4th September, with a delay of two days being caused when two of the forward engines were converted to reverse thrust. This reverse thrust was based on an old Beardmore patent dating to before the Great War and worked on the principle of moving a camshaft to run the opposite way on the valve gear. The R100 had successfully crossed the Atlantic to Canada on her second - hand petrol engines and had shown that the nature of the R101 engine installation was possibly flawed. The Tornadoes had never been flown at full engine power and because of technical problems they had been de-rated to less than 700 H.P. The R101 departed from established British airship practice in her design details. Her fabric was doped before fitting to the airship frame and when she was brought out of the airship shed at Cardington on the morning of Wednesday 1st October 1930 she had been modified structurally. A new forty five foot bay had been fitted between frames eight and nine, just behind the passenger cabin. The new frames were joined by fifteen continuous girders and to prevent the gas bags rubbing against them, they were not spaced equally apart. The R101 was now seven hundred and seventy seven feet long with a gas capacity of five and a half million cubic feet. She rose that evening for her trial up the east coast and returned successfully the next day. This test was considered satisfactory and preparations went ahead for her flight to Karachi, with her departure time set for 7 p.m. on Saturday 4th October. When departure day came around all the passengers had embarked by their allotted time, but there was some delay due to condensation being found in the forward starboard engine. She lifted off at seven thirty six that evening with her Tornadoes running gently, but R101 did not rise smartly as other airships had done. She backed sluggishly and slowly and when she cleared the tower she moved forward very gently, slowly gaining height. At 9 p.m. she was over London with smoke seen to be coming from one of the engine pods. Apparently someone had stood on an oil cooler. She crossed the French coast at around eleven thirty six at Pointe de St. Quentin having travelled about 60 miles. Between one and ten past three in the morning she had only travelled thirty six miles due to strong head winds. Initially these winds were only thirty five miles per hour, but when she was over France they measured fifty five miles per hour. [The Beardmore Tornado had never been run at full power on R101.]

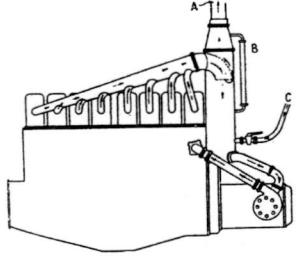

The Tornado cooling system

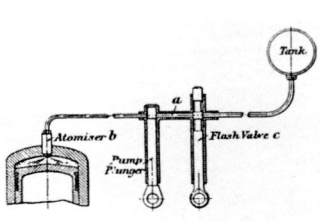

The Tornado ant-flash system

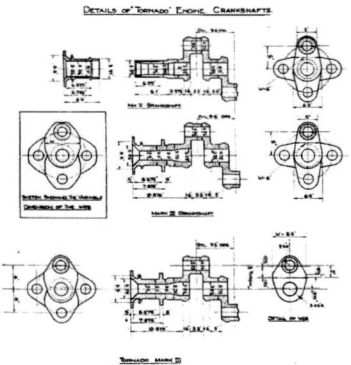

The Tornado crankshaft

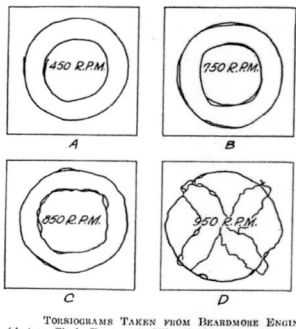

Tornado crankshaft vibration results

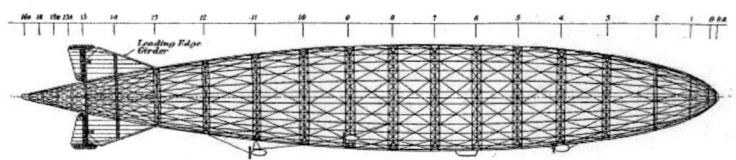

The structure of the R101 showing the Tornado engine pods

 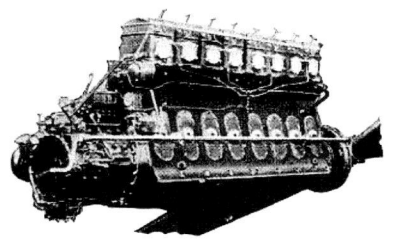

The Tornado MKIII set in its pod   Tornado set with its propeller

The R101 under construction   The gas bag of the R101 partially inflated

The Tornado engines attached to R101   The R101 control cabin

The R101 in flight

The R101 showing five engines

Disaster at Beauvais

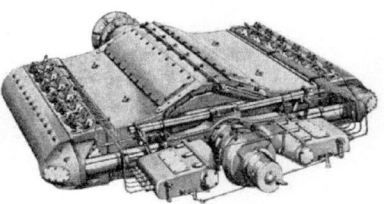
The Beardmore Flat Twelve

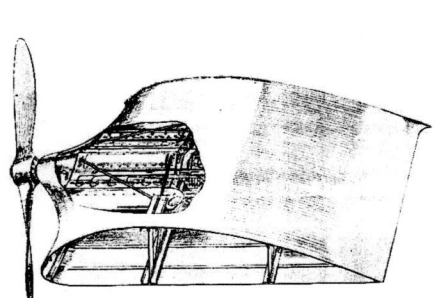
The flat twelve in a flying boat

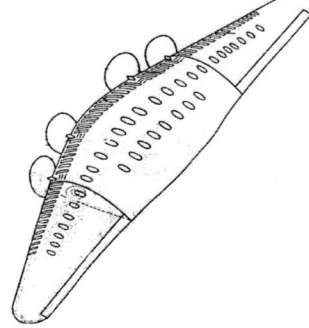
The wing with four flat twelve engines

At three o' clock in the morning the captain called a conference. He felt R101 was flying too low and slow and he gave the order for full power to be applied. When the full power order was being discussed she was flying at her normal cruising speed. It had been hoped that at full power seventy five miles per hour would be reached somewhere along the route of the voyage. Suddenly R101 fell from the sky.

At ten past three in the morning, as he was out hunting rabbits, Monsieur Rabouille from Beauvais witnessed R101 fall from the sky. He heard three explosions, saw the fore part of the airship hit the ground with a crunch and then erupt in flames. R101 hit the ground at between an angle of fifteen and twenty five degrees with her forward engines still turning. Rabouille saw burning figures in the mass of flames. He fled in terror.

The disaster at Beauvais effectively wiped out all the experienced British airship personnel. The saddest loss was that of Major Scott who had been captain of the airship R34 when she had crossed the Atlantic. He was also captain of the later Beardmore built R36 and had married A. J. Campbell's daughter, making the R101's loss all the more painful for Dalmuir. There were only six survivors. The forty eight fatalities were returned to Britain to be buried at Cardington.

A committee was set up to look at the circumstances surrounding the building and flying of the R101. When the committee reported, they found that the Beardmore Tornado was a source of great concern, having never developed its full potential. They found that the ratio of bore to stroke set up unacceptable torsional vibration at 950 r.p.m., which would have meant that the airship would have shaken to bits. To cure this would have meant a complete engine redesign. Beardmore had experimented with a redesigned crankshaft making it stiffer and robust, without success. Another problem was the weight of the Tornado installation, coming in at 17 tons against the 9 tons of R100's. Later in discussions at the Royal Society of Arts, Alan Chorlton felt that the slowness of the combustion of the oil and air inside the engine cylinders at a high compression ratio may have caused the vibration. A sub - report was also requested from the Aeronautical Research Committee who conducted trials with models of the R101. They found that a large rip had formed on her outer cover, caused by severe turbulence and that she had lost gas from number five gas bag when the stormy air gusted in through the torn fabric. Due to these two causes she could not maintain height or lift and this loss of level flight caused her to lose all propeller thrust. Even if she had had full power the propellers would never have been able to develop full thrust due to their flight attitude. The Committee of Inquiry into the loss of the Airship R101 felt that the initial explosion and fire on the R101 was not caused by petrol stored for the starter motors, but by a spark caused by a broken electrical circuit reaching the mixture of hydrogen and air. From the wreck of R101 a surviving Beardmore Tornado was cut from the wreck and presented to the Science Museum, South Kensington, London, where it can still be seen to this day. Even with the company's financial predicaments, the Air Ministry felt that the work Beardmore had done with the Tornado engine was commendable. The development of the fuel pumps which delivered the correct amount of oil to each cylinder was seen as Beardmore's greatest triumph.

For the Air Ministry, the Tornado did not represent the peak of compression ignition development. They had already been looking at a new airship programme. Before the loss of the R101 the Air Ministry had awarded a contract to the E. S. L. Company to develop the Stromboli 1500 H.P. airship engine for airship use. Under test at Farnborough the Stromboli engine kept blowing off its cylinder head due to high pressures in the combustion chamber and even with much redesign the project was cancelled. From 1929 the Beardmore Company made no effort to develop the Tornado engine into other marks for airship use. Beardmore High Speed Diesels were developing a series of rail car engines for railway use, with two being tested by the London Midland Scottish Railway. They even developed a V twelve diesel engine for Canadian National Railways, with possibly a six cylinder model being installed in the Bennie Railplane at Milngavie near Glasgow in 1930. Later plans for a horizontally opposed twelve cylinder diesel engine for aeroplane use were published. This engine had a bore of six inches and a stroke of six and a half inches developing 505 H.P. at 1750 r.p.m. Later on it was to be supercharged with a centrifugal blower, increasing its power to 620 H.P. This engine was shown in a drawing of a flying boat wing and in another drawing of the flying boat, four Tornadoes were shown being fitted. Another American drawing of 1930 showed four Beardmore flat twelve engines installed in a flying wing, but in reality Beardmore were not in a financial position to develop any of these engines. Alan Chorlton left Parkhead in March 1929 after receiving a royalty on all the aero – engines, with the aero-engine division being taken over by Beardmore High Speed Diesels. This Beardmore division remained at Parkhead until 1932 and then moved to Dalmuir in 1933, where they continued manufacturing Beardmore Diesels. In 1936 manufacturing ceased, with the company concentrating its activities as a diesel engine agency, this state of affairs lasting until 1941.

In 1946 a returning soldier wrote to a magazine saying that he had made an astonishing discovery; while travelling in India on a train he had gone through a carriage and noticed an unusual diesel engine. It was very long and had eight cylinders. On one of the plates it had the name "Beardmore." It was a Beardmore Tornado engine, one that had been sent to India as a spare airship engine and had now been fitted to a train.

During a debate in the House of Commons in 1931 the Air Minister was heavily questioned about the loss of the R101. He was asked why she had been built. It was pointed out that the airship was the same length as the Mauritania and only carried a payload of about 40 tons. The minister could not reply. Then he replied to a question on diesel aero-engines. He denied that there was any work being carried out by any company in this country on this type of engine for the Air Ministry or any airship. Consequently, after May 1931, no mention was made of installing Beardmore aero - engines in aircraft or airships

(i)
Post - War Aero - Engines

	Pistons	Bore	Stroke	R.P.M.	Comp. Ratio	H.P.	Weight
Cyclone	6	8.63"	12"	1350	5.25:1	925	2150lbs
Cyclone II	6	8.63"	12"	1350	5.25:1	950	2155lbs
Typhoon	6	8.63"	12"	1400	5.25:1	750	1800lbs
Typhoon II	6	8.63"	12"	1350	5.25:1	800	2233 lbs.
Simoon	8	8.58"	12"	1250	5.25:1	1100	2770lbs
Tornado	8	8.25"	12"	1000	12.25:1	650	4500lbs
Flat Twelve	12	6"	6.5	1750	13.5:1	505	1485 lbs.

(ii)

Air Ministry Contracts
for the Tornado Programme
1929

A.M. 948686 Five sets of atomiser filters
A.M. 937947 Spare parts and tools [ordered twice]
A.M. 931566 Tornado Mk III Engines [cost £7048 . 17s . 10d]

1930

A.M. 957962/29   Fitting Hartzxmark starter
A.M. 4106/30   Fuel pump gear wheel and pinion
A.M. 37361/30   Fitting carburettor and preparing drawings
A.M. 43767/30   Drawings
A.M. 35170/30   Drawings
A.M. 920960/29   Seven - four cylinder starter engines

(iii)

Beardmore Aero - Engines

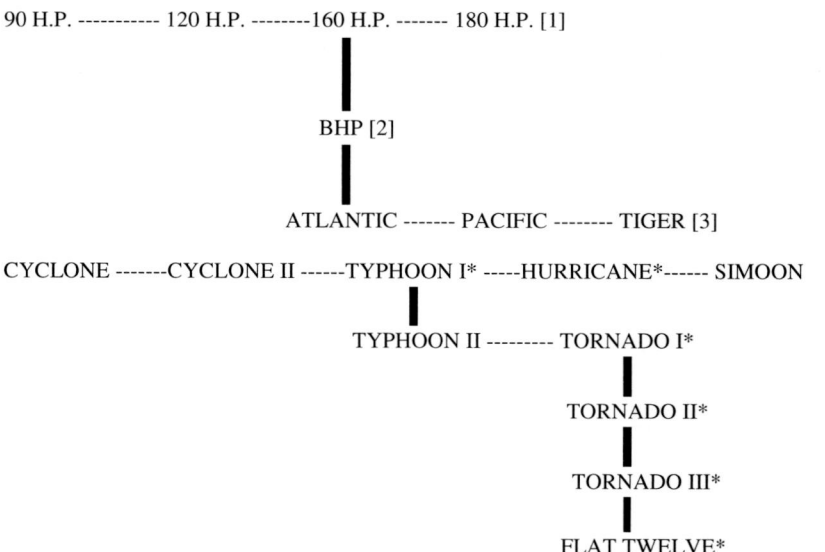

Notes: [1] 120/160 H.P. by Arrol – Johnston/Crossley
       [2] B.H.P. by Galloway /Siddeley Deasy
       [3] Pacific and Tiger by Siddeley Deasy, Atlantic by Galloway
       * Compression Ignition/Diesel

(iv)

R101 Voyages

No.	Date		Duration Hrs.	Mins.
1.	14 - 10 - 29	Round London.	5	38
2.	18 - 10 - 29	Midlands.	9	38
3.	1 - 11 - 29	Norfolk.	7	15
4.	2/3 - 11 - 29	Isle of Wight.	14	2
5.	8 - 11 - 29	Local around Cardington.	3	4
6.	14 - 11 - 29	Local around Cardington.	3	9
7.	17/18 - 11 - 29	England, Scotland, Ireland. [Endurance Flight]	30	41
8.	26 - 6 - 30	Refit Flight.	4	35
9.	27 - 6 - 30	Rehearsal for Display.	12	33
10.	28 - 6 - 30	R.A.F. Display Flight.	12	21
11.	1/2 - 10 - 30	Trial with extra bay.	16	51
12.	4/5 - 10 – 30	Cardington - Beauvais.	7	24

Note: Refit 30 - 11 - 29 to 23 - 6 30, New bay fitted 29 - 6 - 30 to 1 - 10 - 30

(vi)

Propeller Trials for Beardmore Tornado

Type	Date	Place	Remarks
Three Bladed Metal	18 - 2 - 1928	Parkhead	from Rolls-Royce Condor
Two Bladed Hollow Metal	12/13 - 6 - 1928	Parkhead	Also 26 -6 - 26
Wooden Airscrew	28 - 12 - 1928	N/D	"B" Type
Wooden Airscrew	9/10 - 1 - 1929	Farnborough	To Drawing T29243, Type "A", tested to 26 - 1 - 1929
Wooden Airscrew	30 - 1 - 1929	Farnborough	To Drawing T29269, Type "B", tested to 10 - 3 - 29

Note: Tested between February 1928 and March 1929. The wooden propellers were made of Mahogany. Metal airscrews made by Metal Airscrews Ltd.

AIRSHIPS

How the company became involved in airships
Building airships at Inchinnan
A short history of each airship

The main pioneers in airship construction were the Germans, who had their first successful airship flying in 1900. Among the German airship pioneers was Count Ferdinand von Zeppelin, who lent his name to this class of lighter than air craft. At this stage in their development the airships were divided into two distinct classes, rigid airships and non – rigid airships. The non -rigid airship consisted of a shaped gas - bag or balloon, with an underslung car being powered by an engine. On the other hand the rigid airship was quite a different proposition, built with a fabric covered frame around a series of gas bags, with crew accommodation and engines. The rigid airship was commonly known as the Zeppelin while the non – rigid airship was called a Blimp.

1902 saw Britain starting work on its first airships for the British Army and in 1909 a contract was awarded to Vickers to build the first British rigid airship at Barrow. This airship, which was called, "Mayfly," proved to be so heavy that efforts to lighten her caused severe structural weakness and she broke her back on her maiden voyage. The report of the subsequent Court of Inquiry effectively banned the construction of airships in this country for the next two years, but Mayfly gave the infant airship industry experience in working with the new light alloy aircraft metal, Duralumin.

In Britain the proper role for the airship in warfare was seen as reconnaissance and by using the new radio/wireless it would give better communication to the army in the field. The lack of proper hangars and the geography of the British countryside strongly influenced official thinking on the deployment of airships. By 1912 airships were expected to work on the continent with the British Expeditionary Forces and by 1913 there was an increase in the demand for airships. Six were being built in this country, with gas bag volumes varying from 20000 to 208000 cubic feet, with one being built at the Royal Aircraft Factory. The army manoeuvres of 1912 showed the military the value of airships, when two were used during exercises. These were the Beta and the Gamma. On one occasion the Gamma was used for night trials, involving reconnaissance and bomb dropping, but she could not find her landing field in the dark and flew around the East Anglian countryside until she could be recovered at dawn. An important trial for Gamma was her use of radio which could transmit up to a distance of thirty five miles. Though this was an army exercise both airships were crewed by naval personnel. In 1913 the main Admiralty contractor, Vickers, had obtained the plans for the Zeppelin Z IV from Germany and were constructing the airship at Barrow. This airship, later to be called No. 9, took so long to build that she was only ready for service in 1917. Vickers had gone into airship production at Barrow in April 1913, having received the order for No 9 and three non – rigid airships of the Parseval type. Vickers had also obtained the licence to use both the Parseval patents and the metal Duralumin from Germany.

In July 1913 a technical sub - committee reported that airships should be developed in this country, because they could perform long range functions that aeroplanes of those times could not. The committee believed that the Admiralty should take over all the large airships in this country that were being planned or under construction. At the end of 1913 all airships of the Military Wing of the R.F.C. were transferred to the Royal Navy.

On Monday 17th November 1913, at a directors meeting held at Westminster, London the firm of William Beardmore & Co. Ltd., agreed to move into airship construction when they took out an airship patent. This patent was to combine all the advantages of the rigid airship and the non - rigid airship type, without the disadvantages of both. The airship shape was designed around a keel of a tubular inflated structure, which was to be braced internally, with the cars, or gondolas, being suspended in a conventional manner. This patent was never used in Beardmore airships because of the work that was being completed on the airship No 9 by Vickers, Beardmore's partner. Even with this change of plan there is early evidence of airship work being completed at Dalmuir in 1913. In the Beardmore company accounts they had set up a specific ledger account for scrap airships, but nothing survives to indicate the type of work being carried out. When war broke out in 1914, work on No 9 continued until March 1915, when the Admiralty suspended the contract. The chief influence behind this decision was the First Lord of the Admiralty, Winston Churchill, who had little faith in the effectiveness of airships at sea or on land. After he resigned over the debacle of the Dardanelles campaign, the Royal Navy had another look at the airship programme.

A.J. Balfour succeeded Winston Churchill at the Admiralty in May 1915 and by 2nd July 1915 he had decided to restart work on rebuilding airship No 9 and to allow Vickers to build a new class of airship. This new airship class was based on all the experience Vickers had gained with No 9 and was to be called 23 Class. In addition to Vickers, it was decided to employ the resources of Beardmore and Sir W.G. Armstrong, Whitworth & Co. The project leaders were to be Vickers, who would supply the airship contractors with all the bracing stamping and forgings for airship construction. From the beginning, all the firms had great difficulty with production, since they had little experience in working with the new airship type, though Beardmore provided all the fabric, gas bags and mechanical gear for their airships. Of the six airships of this 23 class, Beardmore were to build two, No 24 and No 27. This order for the first two Beardmore airships was confirmed by the Admiralty during January 1916.

The chief skill which Beardmore was able to develop in airships was in the design and manufacture of the airship gas - bags. The bags were made of single ply cotton, painted on one side with rubber, and then lined with a layer of goldbeaters' skins which was varnished on completion. It was women munitions workers who were used to apply the goldbeater's skins inside the gas bag before it was completed. The company went on to develop glues which would help the skins stick more efficiently to the cotton bags. One type of glue was patented. The Ioco works at Anniesland in the west end of Glasgow provided all the airship outer cloth, which was a weave of two ply rubberised cotton. This was used for the airship nose, while a single - ply was used for the rest of the structure.

Design of the British airship progressed slowly until the night of 23rd - 24th September 1916 when the German Zeppelin L33 was brought down. The wreck of L33 was inspected by the Director of Naval Construction, who felt that the German design was in some ways better than those of British airships still on the drawing board and at the construction stage, so it was decided that Britain should go German.

The 23 Class of airship was found to be really only suitable for training purposes, local patrol and convoy work. The Royal Navy wanted an airship to have a range of two thousand miles for naval patrol and reconnaissance work and be able to work with the Grand Fleet. For war service it was recommended that there should be an airship fleet of sixteen airships, based on the L33 Zeppelin. With the approval of this scheme Beardmore received the order in November 1916 to commence building the R34 and by January 1917 had received provisional orders for three more airships R36, R40 and R41.

The surviving evidence would seem to suggest that Beardmore were not happy with the profitability of airship orders, even though the building of the Inchinnan works and provision of capital equipment was heavily subsidised by the Admiralty. Dalmuir had initially provided all the airship work for the first of the airships, but with the Armistice in 1918 all airship production had been transferred from Dalmuir to Inchinnan. At the end of the war there were five British rigid airships in commission, with eleven under construction and by that time it was felt at the Admiralty that British airships could be compared to, or were even better than, the German Zeppelins. At the Armistice there were four firms engaged in airship work; Vickers, Armstrong Whitworth, Beardmore and Short. Throughout the war the design and supply of airships was controlled by two heads of Admiralty departments, the Director of Air Services, with the Assistant Superintendent of Airships being responsible for supply. By October 1919 airships became the responsibility of the Air Ministry, who displayed little enthusiasm for the type. By April 1921 the government had stopped all development work on airships and was prepared to sell all the survivors to anyone who was willing to fly them commercially.

BEARDMORE AIRSHIPS

No 24

This airship was the second of the 23 Class and was built with a striking external keel for strength. Her frames and structure were initially assembled at Dalmuir, with final assembly taking place at Inchinnan. She had a cubic capacity of nearly one million cubic feet and was commissioned at the east coast airship station of East fortune on 28th October 1917, at a cost of £161683. No 24 was not regarded as a very successful craft because she was overweight, this resulted in the removal of one engine from her rear cab making her three engined. She was used partly for training and convoy patrol and on occasion for mooring tests. No 24 flew a total of 164 hours two minutes and was finally dismantled for scrap at Pulham, Norfolk, in December 1919.

Specification

Volume: 940000 cubic feet
Length: 535'
Max Diameter: 53'

Engines: 4 X 250 H.P. Rolls - Royce
Useful Lift: 6 tons
Trial speed: 55 M.P.H.

No 27

When no 27 was laid down at Inchinnan on 16 March 1917 she was built at a time of great shortages of engines, metal, wood and skilled labour. At that time it was taking the Germans an average of ten weeks to build a Zeppelin, while in Britain the average time was one year. The designation R for rigid in airship nomenclature was introduced to British airships after the 18th December 1918 .When 27 was commissioned at Inchinnan on 29th June 1918 she had become airship R 27. She was built at a cost of £131321 but was destroyed in a petrol spillage accident at Howden after flying only ninety hours.

Specification

Volume: 990600 cubic feet
Length: 539 '
Max Diameter: 53'

Engines: 4 X 250 H.P. Rolls - Royce
Useful Lift: 8 tons
Trial speed: 56.5 m.p.h

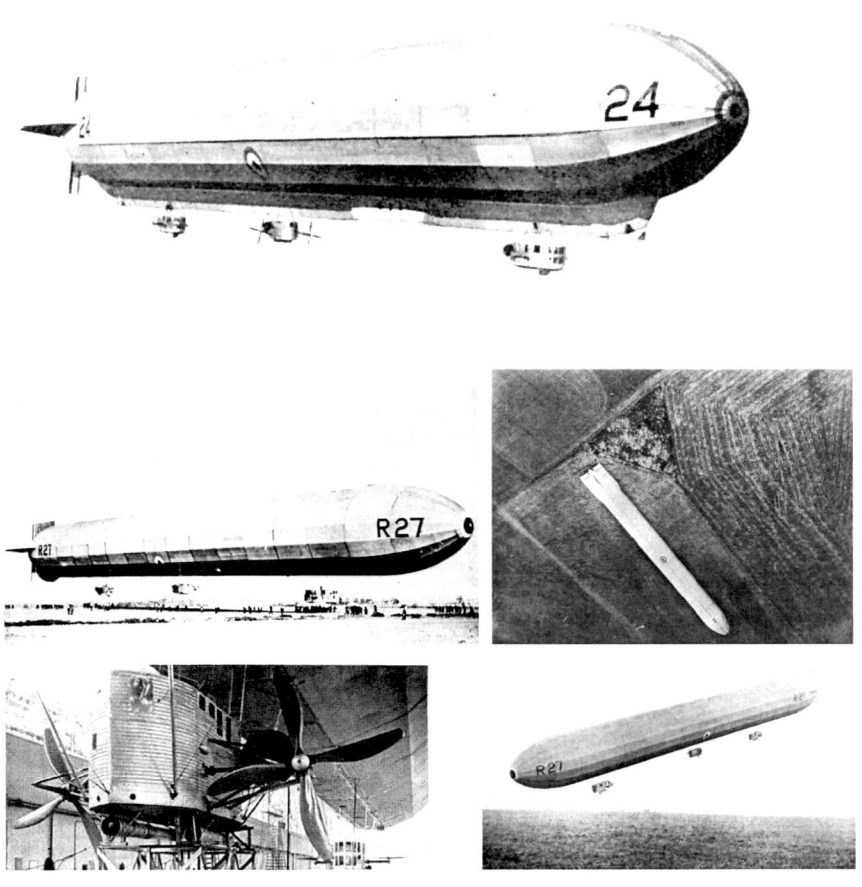

Above are views of the Beardmore R24/R27 class including the control cabin

R 34

On the night of 23rd - 24th September 1916 three Super – Zeppelins, L31, L32 and L33, set out to attack London. L31, superbly handled flew straight over the city dropping flares, she then flew through cloud cover, dropped her bombs, dodged the searchlights and flew home. L32 was not so fortunate. As she flew over Billericay she was attacked by a B.E 2c night fighter and shot down in flames. Fortune did not favour L33, for while she was over London she was attacked by another B.E 2c flown by Lt. Brandon, and then hit by anti - aircraft fire. Bocker, her captain, decided to fly her back towards the continent, but she was losing gas and height and rather than be lost at sea, he decide to turn back to England. There she force-landed near a cottage. Her crew destroyed the ammunition then set fire to the airship to try and destroy it. This they failed to do. They could not raise the occupants of the cottage and had to surrender to a village policeman. As for L33, she was inspected and found to be in excellent condition resulting in all British airship construction being halted with production concentrating on copies of L33.

Zeppelin L33 crashed and burned out notice the cottage

In November 1917 Beardmore were contracted by the Admiralty to build the R34, a copy of the crashed Zeppelin L33. She was laid down at Inchinnan on 9th December 1917 and made her first voyage on 14th March 1919. Before she was walked out of the Inchinnan airship shed, her gas bags were inflated with hot air to test for leaks and then inflated partially with hydrogen. Under Captain Scott she completed her proving flights around Glasgow and Loch Lomond, flying down to the Isle of Man then back to Scotland. During March 1919 an invitation was received from the Aero -Club of America proposing that the R 34 fly across the Atlantic to America. Even though she had been designed for working in the North Sea, it was decided by the Admiralty that she should go. Before her trip was to take place she was armed and sent around the Baltic States for a further proving flight of 54 hours, after which she returned to her base at East Fortune. On 2nd July 1919 she left East Fortune for the first ever crossing of the Atlantic by airship. Along her route the Admiralty had posted warships in the event of a disaster and reflecting her North Sea specification, she arrived at New York, low on fuel, mainly caused by diverting from a thunderstorm. Her trip lasted 108 hours twelve minutes; just five hours short of a normal sea voyage and when she prepared to land one of her officers parachuted to the ground to arrange docking. R 34 returned to Britain on the 13th July 1919 after a three day flight across the Atlantic. Due to weather conditions at East Fortune she was diverted to Pulham in Norfolk. She did not take to the air again until February 1920 and then there was a delay of nearly another year when she took to the air again at Howden airship station. On 27th January 1921, while flying from Howden air station she struck a hill, severely damaging her nose and forward structure. R 34 was assessed as being beyond economical repair and subsequently scrapped.

R34 under construction at Inchinnan   R34 walked out at Inchinnan

R34 being readied for flight

R34 control cabin

Tail of the R34 in America

R34 being readied for flight

Captain Scott

Over the Renfrewshire countryside R34 in the air

Losing ballast in America Spectators at Mineola N.Y.

R34 tied down at Mineola N.Y.

R34 nose view, company shield apparent Over Newfoundland

R34 over the English countryside at Pulham

The crashed R34 after its flight from Howden

R 34 Specification

Volume: 1950000 cubic feet **Length:** 643' **Diameter:** 78' 9"
Engines: 5 x 250 H.P. Sunbeam Maori **Lift:** 16 tons

R 36

After completing airship R 34 work commenced immediately on the next Beardmore airship, R 36. It was decided that she be fitted out for civilian work and all her military specifications were deleted. She was fitted with an external cabin, which was electrically heated for fifty passengers. Work on her was completed at Inchinnan during April 1921 and she was the final airship completed there. Due to official apathy, R 36 made few flights, one of which was to direct the traffic at the Ascot races on 14th June 1921. On 17th June 1921 she returned to her berth at Pulham, but unfortunately struck the mooring mast and became unairworthy. With a change in the weather it was decided to berth her in the airship shed. However this was easier said than done.

The shed was occupied by the Zeppelin L 64 which was quickly dismantled, but as R 36 was being prepared to move inside the shed she struck the shed and was damaged. Due to the economic climate of the times all repair work on her was suspended and she was placed in store. Official interest in her rekindled in 1924 and she was taken in hand as the trial ship for the new airship programme. It was hoped to fly her out to Egypt as the pathfinder for the R 101, but even though she was repaired she never flew again. Of all the airships that had been built in Great Britain, R 36 is considered by many to be the most aerodynamically pleasing and most commercially viable of the whole class, but that did not stop her being broken up in 1926.

Specification
Volume: 195600 cubic feet. **Length:** 675' **Lift:** 16 tons **Diameter:** 84' 9"
Engines: 3 x 250 h.p sunbeam Cossacks and 2 x Maybach engines from Zeppelin L 71

R36 being completed at Inchinnan, engine pod and passenger cabin

Inside the Inchinnan airship shed on the verge of completion

R36 over the airship sheds at Inchinnan Scotland

R36 attached to the airship mast after a test flight

Kite Balloons

On the outbreak of the Great War the main British artillery spotting balloon was in the process of being replaced by aeroplanes. But wartime conditions in the field proved that there was still a military requirement for the captive balloon. Before the war, Captain Parseval of the German Army had developed the Drachen, which was essentially a sausage shaped gas bag with a large air inflated tail acting as a rudder and preventing the balloon from rotating. The British now formulated a requirement for a captive balloon, which was met by the Belgians. The Belgians, after their retreat from their homeland, had only one of three Drachens left, which was quickly copied, becoming the British Drachen Kite Balloon. Though an improvement on the old type of spherical balloon, the Drachen was unwieldy, tended to use a taught anchor cable and was very labour intensive.

During the autumn of 1916 the first French Caquot kite balloons arrived in this country. Essentially similar to the Drachen, with a wrap round tail, it was much more streamlined in shape. It was designed for all the opposite reasons to the Drachen; it was economic in the use of manpower, it did not use a taught anchor cable and was much more stable in the air. This balloon was chosen by the Admiralty for fitting to ships and Captain Caquot came over from France to modify it further. Three fins replaced the wrap round tail, which were set at an angle of one hundred and twenty degrees, making it more stable. By December 1916 Dalmuir received an order for twelve Caquot kite balloons, with one being partially completed in December. They were fitted to all classes of warships from battleships to trawlers and for night work they were fitted with a flare underneath the observer's basket. For sea duties the Caquot carried two observers connected to the ship by telephone and for anti - submarine work it was flown at an altitude of between five hundred and one thousand feet. For naval gunfire spotting the ship would anchor two miles off shore and the Caquot would be let up to two thousand feet before spotting would commence. On one occasion during an anti - submarine duty it required ten ships with ten Caquots to track one submarine, with negligible results. On 12th July 1917 a Caquot flown off H.M.S. Patriot spotted U 69, which was duly sunk.

   When manufactured at Dalmuir the Caquots were made of yellow dyed cotton, painted aluminium. The balloons used standard airship fabric which came in rolls of fifty, eighty or one hundred yards in length, with an average width of thirty six to forty inches. The demand for kite balloons, in 1917, was about twenty three a week rising to eighty five a week by 1918 but due to shortages of material only eight balloons were being produced weekly overall. Records are not clear as to how many Caquots were produced at Dalmuir, but using Air Ministry accounts set against the price produced by Beardmore, only four kite balloons were made.

   With a post - war review of Admiralty requirements on capital ships it was felt that the anti - submarine kite balloon was a failure. All the kite balloons were removed from the ships, but the winches and associated equipment were retained. For training duties at Roehampton the Royal Navy used the old spherical balloon. There are few details of the Beardmore supplied spherical balloon.

The Parseval Drache with German observers   A French Army Caquot tied down

The Caquot observation balloon on land and ship

The Caquot winch and crew, the winch was installed on naval vessels

H.M.S. Argus
Evolution of the aircraft carrier
Testing H.M.S. Argus, Chanak Crisis
Deployment to China, Squadrons on board
The Second World War

In December 1912, William Beardmore & Co. Ltd., of the Dalmuir Naval Construction Works, submitted to the Admiralty a design for, "Parent Ship for Naval Aeroplanes and Torpedo - Boat Destroyers". This ship had been designed for the Marquis of Graham who had seen the potential of aeroplanes on ships and had submitted the plans. The vessel was to displace 15000 tons with a length of 430 feet, a speed of fifteen knots and beam on the waterline of 82 feet. On top of the hull was a flight deck 450 feet long, with a width of 110 feet. Along each side of the deck were, "side houses," 220 feet long, through which the funnels and ventilators passed. Inside the side houses were six hangars for aeroplanes with their wings spread and twin cranes, which could lift four aeroplanes from the forward hangars with their wings folded. Hinged, inclined gates were provided between the deckhouses. These were about 50 feet wide. When landing on the quarterdeck an aeroplane could very well end up at the gates. The design of this ship was very carefully considered by the Admiralty, but it was rejected because the Royal Navy had little experience of working with aeroplanes at sea. However the Beardmore concept was not dead with the Admiralty's rejection, for in the Naval Estimates of 1914 – 15, £81000 had been allocated for a new seaplane ship. This vessel's construction had been anticipated by the purchase in 1913 of H.M.S. Ark Royal, a former collier built at the Blyth Shipbuilding Company. As a seaplane carrier she did not have a flight deck, but stowed her aeroplanes in a large hold and when flying the aircraft off, she had to stop, lift them by crane out of the hangar and place them in the water. Clearly she was to give the R.N.A.S. that much needed experience of working with aeroplanes at sea.

 When war broke out in 1914, Dalmuir was working on a vessel, contract number 519, which was a liner for the Lloyd Sabuado Line of Genoa, Italy and built as the "Conte Rosso" for the South American run. Work had started on her around June 1914, when her keel was laid down. William Beardmore had acquired a large portion of shares in Lloyd Sabuado and had used his influence to have the liner built at Dalmuir. Even with the unfavourable production conditions with the outbreak of war, work on her hull continued into 1915.

   In August 1916 the Admiralty decided to purchase the hull of the incomplete liner Conte Rosso and have her converted into a seaplane carrier as H.M.S. Argus. The completion of the vessel was strongly influenced by the 1912 design of the Marquis of Graham and became the starting point for the conversion programme. Commander G.R.A. Holmes was designated by the Admiralty as the liaison officer between the Air Department, the Director of Naval Construction and Beardmore. Due to the advanced stage in the building of her hull, it was not possible to redesign the vessel for high speed, which was necessary for her to work with units of the Grand Fleet. Modifications were made which increased her speed from eighteen knots to twenty and three quarter knots for short periods in a normal sea and twenty knots for rough conditions. The original "Conte Rosso" structure and deck were retained, up to the shelter deck, which became the floor of the aeroplane hangar and, above the shelter deck, a hangar was provided with workshops, stores and a flying off deck. Aeroplanes of those days were seen as an aid to reconnaissance. It was as eyes that the aircraft were planned and designed and it was these eyes that the Royal Navy needed in H.M.S. Argus.

   To find out the effects of air flow over the deck houses, a quarter scale model of her was made at the National Physical Laboratory, Teddington. These tests proved that to have the minimum air disturbance over the ship, the space between the hangar roof and the deck should be made as wide as possible. This meant that the side houses were deleted, one already having been fitted as she was being completed. The hangar roof was then strengthened with steel to take the stress of the flying off deck by the installation of expansion joints and a light lattice framework. Tests at the laboratory also found that the hot exhaust gasses from the funnels would seriously disturb the air over the flight deck and around her stern. This meant that all her funnels were discarded to be replaced by horizontal ducting which discharged the exhaust gas astern of the ship. Electric fans of 74 horse power and 117 inches in diameter were installed underneath the exhaust and connected by ducting to the horizontal funnels. If one funnel was put out of action the gasses could then be diverted through the other funnel. Beardmore installed a telegraph indicator for the bridge, which was repeated in the engine room and showed the Captain or Engineer Officer what position the fans were in, or whether they were running or not. Inside her hull she had a hangar 330 feet long, 68 feet wide and with a height of 48 feet, with provision for twenty aeroplanes. The hangar was split into four working spaces by fireproof curtains, with the port side having heaters, radiators and racks for torpedoes. Overhead were rails for transporting aeroplanes and along the starboard side were store rooms for spares. Ahead of the hangar were the workshops. There were two electric lifts initially installed. The aft one was sixty feet by eighteen feet and the forward one was 30 feet by 36 feet. Seaplanes were recovered by two electric cranes at her stern and when aircraft were stored on deck they were protected by a fourteen foot wooden screen which could be raised or lowered. Armament consisted of four four inch dual purpose and two four inch quick firing guns. Her machinery was of Parsons steam turbines, arranged in a series of four shafts, with her boilers being six double - ended and six single ended types, producing 20500 horse power. The chart house was made retractable to give a clear flight deck and was raised by hydraulic power. There was no familiar bridge on H.M.S. Argus. Commander Holmes was the genius behind the Argus conversion and she owed more to him above the hangar deck than the Beardmore concern. Events in the evolution of the ship were once again taken out of her control.

The original aircraft carrier designed by the Marquis of Graham

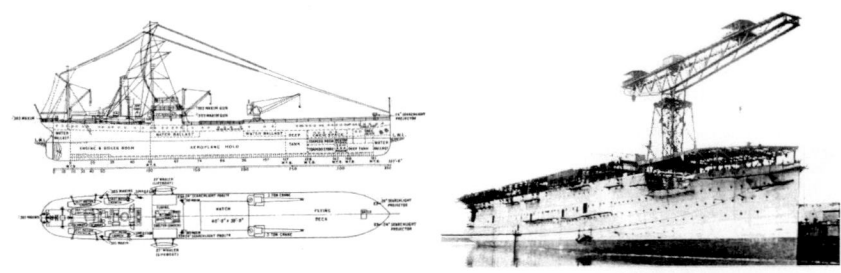

H.M.S. Ark Royal   H.M.S. Argus on the verge of completion

Argus at Dalmuir July 1918 a Sopwith Strutter is on the flight deck

Re - fitting the Whiteway arrester gear off the Burntisland Roads

On 25th September 1917 Admiral Beatty was sent proposals for expanding the air cover of the Grand Fleet and one of the proposals was to convert H.M.S. Argus from a seaplane carrier to an aircraft carrier, carrying torpedo carrying aeroplanes. Even before Admiral Beatty had received these plans, he had sent the Admiralty his ideas for an aircraft policy for the Grand Fleet. By the 17th October a new Grand Fleet aircraft plan was drawn up and it was felt that no decision could be made as to the exact deployment of H.M.S. Argus as a torpedo - plane carrier. Out of this plan came a project to attack German ships and harbour installations at Kiel with a Sopwith torpedo carrying aeroplane, later to be called the Sopwith Cuckoo. On 16th January 1918, after considering a memo from the First Sea Lord, Admiral Sir Rosslyn Wemyss, it was proposed to keep the seaplane carrier H.M.S. Campania until the completion of fly off deck trials on H.M.S. Argus. The reconstruction of H.M.S. Argus, Ex Conte Rosso, took longer than expected, due to shortages of steel and skilled labour.

On 4th July 1918, Thomas N.S. Dickson of Beardmore was granted a patent on an improved method of ship construction. The patent described how a ship was to be built to a special method of cold rolling the steel plates around the ship frames. This resulted in a ship hull which was truly perpendicular in cross section and from all accounts this method of construction was incorporated into the Conte Rosso and continued into the completion of H.M.S. Argus.

H.M.S. Argus was commissioned by Captain H.H. Smith D.S.O., R.N., at nine o' clock in the morning, Saturday 14th September 1918 and two hours later she was joined at Dalmuir Dock by her crew from Devonport Barracks. On Monday, 16th September, she started her steam trials, at varying speeds and these were carried out over the measured mile off Arran. Before she sailed she had embarked a single Sopwith One and a Half Strutter and along her deck she had the Whiteway arrester gear taken from the hybrid battlecruiser/aircraft carrier H.M.S. Furious. After completing her steam trials, she left the Clyde from Greenock, for the Burntisland Roads, on Saturday 21st September at twenty past five in the morning and sailed around Scotland, arriving on the Firth of Forth the next day. At Burntisland she was prepared for flying experiments under the direction of Commander Bell - Davis, V.C., R.N. The trials were to take place in three phases; the first phase was to find the correct landing and taking off positions on the deck and the correct landing speed; the second phase was to try out actual deck landing and the third and final phase, to test how the arrester gear would work.

On Tuesday 24th September 1918, at half past four in the afternoon, off the Burntisland Roads, two Sopwith Strutters, flown by Commander Bell - Davis and Captain L.H. Cockey from Turnhouse, flew low over H.M.S. Argus. The aeroplanes then landed on and off thirteen times and to assist the pilots on landing, Bell - Davis had marked the deck with red markings. The first run was made into a wind of twenty two knots, with H.M.S. Argus steaming at fifteen knots and proved that aeroplanes could land safely on her deck. After each Sopwith landed it was taxied over her deck, under perfect control, but it was felt that the arrester gear would be better placed well forward, towards the bow, which would help the pilot control the aircraft. The tests continued and on Thursday 26th September, 21 landings and take offs were made with the same two pilots and aeroplanes. Bell - Davis now felt that the best wind speed for landing was twenty five knots. To slow the aeroplanes down further, he fitted gymnastic mats under the arrester wires. After going into Rosyth Dockyard to have a dummy bridge and superstructure fitted to her starboard side she was once again off Burntisland on 1st October, with Rear Admiral Phillimore to witness the trials. Bell - Davis flew off and on three times that day. These tests proved to be the very first landing and take - offs by an aeroplane at sea, on a moving ship. By 21st October she had two further trials aircraft embarked, a Sopwith Pup and a Sopwith Camel. The Pup, flown by two pilots, Lt. Arnold and Commander Bell - Davis, had the modified Busteed skid undercarriage and airscrew guard. Unfortunately, during the trials, the Camel fell into the sea, the pilot being rescued. On 6th November a Sopwith Cuckoo had been flown off for the first time carrying a torpedo and on Armistice Day, Monday 11th November 1918, she was still on trials. By December 1918, 185 Squadron, Royal Air force, was embarked, but the war was over and the attack on the German Fleet at Kiel was quietly forgotten.

The first landings and take offs by Bell Davis from Turnhouse

The elevating bridge   Sopwith Cuckoo torpedo bomber

Interior of the hangar with Cuckoos   The Parnell Panther

A Pup on landing trials   A 2F-1 Camel makes an approach

Stern view showing open deck   Argus with H.M.S Hermes at a royal review

Argus leaves Malta for Turkey

Fairey Flycatchers from H.M.S. Argus

Owing to the high wastage of aeroplanes crash landing on H.M.S. Furious it was decided to withdraw her from the Grand Fleet and replace her with H.M.S. Argus. A few landings were made on her deck without the use of any arrester gear, but it was decided to retain the fore and aft system of wires over her deck. To slow the aeroplanes down further, the wires were then placed over her lift, which was lowered nine inches, with sloping ramps at either end. When an aircraft landed it dropped into the well and pushed the undercarriage spreader hooks onto the wires, preventing it from going up the other side. After initial testing the system was judged a success and retained by H.M.S. Argus for the Atlantic Fleets' cruise to the Mediterranean in 1920. On this cruise many landings were made in rough weather under operational conditions and many of them were crashes, not landings. During one exercise there were 25 landings on her deck of which twelve were crashes, but it was felt that this was due to the narrowness of the deck. The landing wires were then modified and placed over her complete deck. Later in the year she had accepted 500 landings, with only one machine going over the side, but of these landings 40 were write - offs and 90 involved minor damage. Clearly this sort of attrition was unacceptable and other ways of landing were investigated.

   The Admiralty felt that the straight edge of the landing on deck, at the stern, was a source of accidents and they had it modified. The straight edge was now rounded down which meant that larger and faster aeroplanes could now land safely. Landing on an aircraft carrier was now like landing on an aerodrome, with the pilot bringing the aeroplane on to land on a centre line. Aircraft were now no longer hampered by all the gear necessary for the fore and aft landing wires, such as propeller guards and spreader bar hooks, which meant that the Whiteway Arrester Gear could be dispensed with. These advances on carrier construction meant that H.M.S. Argus could now be used as a trials ship until the newer aircraft carriers, H.M.S. Hermes and H.M.S. Eagle, could join the fleet.

   During January 1921 the Air Ministry purchased the Vickers Viking amphibian which had won its class in the 1920 air competition. As N147 it was embarked on H.M.S. Argus for proving trials and was given an armament of twin Lewis machine guns and two 100 pound bombs. Even though the trials went smoothly, the Vickers Viking was not adopted for carrier or capital ship use. Another aeroplane which was tested was the Blackburn Dart which went through its trials at the end of October 1921 and was adopted as the fleet's standard single seat torpedo bomber. A very popular aeroplane, it had a reputation as being easy to land on a carrier deck and deliveries commenced during March 1922.

Turkey, as one of Germany's allies, had been heavily defeated during the Great War and had lost territory to its old enemy, Greece. Britain, as one of the victorious powers maintained a neutral zone around the Dardanelles and its base of operations was Chanak on the Asia Minor side of Turkey. Turkey attacked Greece and its armies threatened the garrison at Chanak. On 18th September 1922 H.M. Argus sailed from Portsmouth and headed for the Dardanelles. With her she took six crated Nieuport Nightjars of 203 Squadron from R.A.F. Leuchars, together with eleven Fairey IIId. When she arrived at Malta on 23rd September she picked up another six Fairey seaplanes and two days later she was in the Dardanelles. The Nightjars were flown to Kilya airfield, across the narrows of the Dardanelles, opposite Chanak, while the Fairey IIIds were beached in Kilya Bay. On the 10th - 11th October further reinforcements arrived with H.M.S. Ark Royal, which was carrying the Bristol Fighters of 4 Squadron. H.M.S. Ark Royal tied up beside H.M.S. Argus and, during the night, the aeroplanes were transferred to her flight deck. By morning the Bristol Fighters were ready to fly off and in the afternoon H.M.S. Argus sailed into the wind with all twelve aeroplanes taking off and landing at Kilya Airfield. The Chanak Crisis did not resolve itself until well into 1923. On 20th December 1922, H.M.S. Argus left for home waters to pay off for a refit. Early in 1923 she was once again being used as a trials ship for the Air Ministry. She tested two aeroplanes, the Fairey Flycatcher and the Parnal Plover. The latter was not all that successful with only a limited number being ordered, but the Flycatcher was reported as being ideal for carrier use and served with the Royal Navy's carrier fleet until being declared obsolete in 1935. H.M.S. Argus was refitted at Chatham during 1925 – 26, when an opportunity was taken to fit her with anti - torpedo bulges, altering her breadth to 75 feet nine inches beam over fenders and ninety one foot six inches over her lifeboats. These bulges extended from frame four to frame nineteen, which was just below the exhaust fans and also helped to improve her sea keeping qualities. After 1926 she was allocated to the Atlantic Fleet.

In January 1927 she left the UK for China, carrying two flights of Fairey IIIDs and a flight of Fairey Flycatchers. Her first port of call, in February 1927, was Hong Kong, with her aircraft operating from the race track, which later became Kai Tak airport. On 23rd March 1927 she was off Shanghai. As she docked she was involved in a naval action with a Chinese destroyer and a battery of guns on a fort, the Chinese destroyer using her for cover during the action. There were anxious moments before she anchored off the Shanghai Bund. On 14th April her aircraft were taken by road to the Shanghai recreation ground. When the aircraft took off they had to swing over Shanghai and towards the French Concession, avoiding the conflict between the warring Chinese. The Chinese had never seen aircraft so close and flooded the streets when the aircraft took off and landed. They stood on the roofs of the houses and in the streets to watch. By September 1927 the situation had stabilised and H.M.S. Argus returned to British waters, leaving a small detachment to set up base facilities at Kai Tak.

By 1929 she was back in home waters, operating, in addition to Flycatchers and Blackburns, the fleet's new Fairey IIIf. Fitted with floats the Fairey IIIfs were recovered from the sea using a mat towed behind the ship, with the aeroplanes being recovered by her after cranes.

Crashed Blackburn Blackburn N9826

Argus in the Dardanelles

Bristol Fighters on board and readied to fly off

Nightjars at Chanak ready to fly offVickers Viking

Fairey IIId on floats

Blackburns in flight and on the Argus stern

H.M.S. Argus at Rosyth for refit   A familiar view of H.M.S. Argus

Fairy IIId is hoisted aboard   Fairey IIIf in flight near Wemyss Bay

Blackburn Dart the Sopwith Cuckoo replacement

Fairey IIIf's in flight target towing

Fairey IIIf on floats

Argus derelict before her major refit

Argus lowers a seaplane at Shanghai

Argus on her way to Shanghai

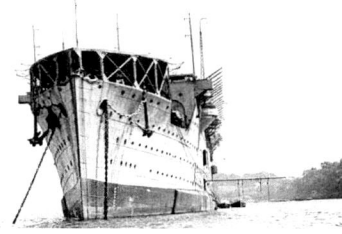
A bow view showing the support lattice

Argus alongside at Shanghai

In 1932 she was placed in reserve at Rosyth and four years later, in July 1936, she was taken in hand for a refit at Devonport Dockyard for an extensive modernisation programme. Her boilers were replaced using scrap destroyer machinery, her four inch armament was suppressed and the forward deck was rebuilt and strengthened to take a catapult. Her bow was widened by five feet and her deck levelled. She was still at Devonport in December 1937 and was due to complete her fitting out as a target aeroplane carrier in the summer of 1938. The delay in having her ready for service was due to the slow progress in fitting her machinery and the delivery of structural material. During the spring of 1939 she served in the Mediterranean with a Fleet Requirements Unit Target Facilities Flight, with a photographic interpreters unit on board but returned to home waters to pay off into reserve at Portsmouth for a new role that of training carrier.

With the appointment of Winston Churchill as First Lord of The Admiralty on the outbreak of the Second World War, one of his first decisions was to arrange for H.M.S. Argus to be sent to the Mediterranean as a training carrier. He had seen her earlier at Portsmouth and made enquiries about her condition and deployment.

He was told that she was a strong ship and that her hull was in perfect condition and required little in the way of modification for wartime duties. Churchill recommended that she be recommissioned immediately, using the surviving crew from the sunken carrier, H.M.S. Courageous. As the autumn of 1939 moved into one of the coldest winters in living memory, H.M.S. Argus sailed to the French port of Toulon in the Mediterranean. Her aircraft, fourteen yellow painted Fairey Swordfish, operated from the air base at Hyeres, near Toulon and made over 2000 deck landings, with 103 Swordfish pilots and 83 fighter pilots qualifying as carrier pilots. Then Germany attacked and France fell. Italy, seeing the plight of France under German attack, declared war on France and Britain and invaded Southern France. The reply of the Fleet Air Arm was swift; the Swordfish bombed Genoa on the 14th June 1940 and were then ordered home. The squadron split; half returned to Britain, while the other half flew to Malta to become the island's strike force. H.M.S. Argus returned home to Britain with a new role that of aircraft transport.

On 31st July she sailed from Gibraltar with H.M.S. Ark Royal, Valiant, Resolution and the two cruisers, H.M.S. Enterprise and Arethusa, for Operation Hurry. This operation had started on 18th July when R.A.F. aircrew, all with carrier experience, gathered at R.A.F. Uxbridge. From there they moved to Abbotsinch to form 401 Flight with twelve Hurricanes. H.M.S. Argus had dry - docked at Govan on 17th June 1940 at ten twenty six in the evening and there she took on the Hurricanes of 401 Flight. On 20th July she left Govan at two thirty three in the morning and at half past six in the evening of the 24th July she sailed from the "Tail o' the Bank," bound for Gibraltar.

When the fleet cleared Gibraltar they were bombed by Italian aircraft, but no ships were damaged. On 2nd August, eighty miles south west of Sardinia, the Hurricanes flew off and two hours and fifty minutes later they all landed safely at Malta. There, the Hurricanes formed 216 Squadron and became a vital part of the defence of the island.

Takoradi was a port in the Gold Coast, now Ghana and from there it was decided that Royal Air force units in Egypt would be resupplied with aeroplanes which would fly from there across the continent.

H.M.S. Argus arrived at Takoradi on 5th September 1940 and her thirty Hurricanes were ready to go the next day. On the way to the Gold Coast she was the escort to the Middle East convoy A.P. 2, as far as Freetown. Her most unhappy resupply took place two months later; it was once again decided to resupply Malta with a force of Hurricane fighters. Twelve Hurricanes flew off her deck with only four arriving, eight being lost in the sea. There had been confusion over navigation and the pilots had not been trained properly. When Churchill heard of this he vowed it would never happen again. After this operation, H.M.S. Argus returned to the Clyde as training carrier, but left as part of the escort to convoy W.S. 5A, carrying the Swordfish of 825 Squadron. This convoy was attacked by the German cruiser Hipper on Christmas morning, with one ship being slightly damaged. She went as far as Gibraltar, then returned to the Clyde in January 1941. By now Churchill had become Prime Minister and Minister of Defence and took a further interest in the activities of H.M.S. Argus. He wanted her to become part of a U - Boat hunting group and he suggested that three groups be formed, but this suggestion was never carried out. In the spring of 1941 H.M.S. Argus accompanied H.M.S. Ark Royal on another Malta re - supply operation and in May she covered troop convoy W.S. 8B as far as Gibraltar. That May she had embarked Fairey Fulmars of 800Y Squadron for fleet fighter duties to Malta and the Swordfish of 812 Squadron. After this operation she was back on the Firth of Clyde for more deck training.

Events in Eastern Europe were to change the pattern of her voyages for this part of the war. On Saturday 21st July 1941 Germany attacked the Soviet Union and Churchill pledged support. 151 Wing, consisting of 81 and 134 Hurricane Squadrons, was formed to give fighter protection to the Soviet Naval Base of Murmansk in Northern Russia. H.M.S. Argus had been dry docked at Barclay Curle's yard at Elderslie, on the Clyde, for a refit on 17th June, but she was now allocated to the Murmansk operation, called Operation Benedict. On the 28th July crews once again arrived at Abbotsinch to train on how to fly off Hurricanes. from a carrier. The crews embarked at Gourock and headed for Scapa Flow and in the holds of the accompanying merchant ships were another 200 Hurricanes for the Soviet Air force. When H.M.S. Argus arrived off Russia on 7th September she flew off twenty four Hurricanes in four flights of six aircraft, commencing with 134 Squadron. To defend the carrier she had embarked two Grumman Martlet fighter aircraft from H.M.S. Audacity, the first escort carrier. These fighters, which were struck below deck when the Hurricanes flew off, were not used, since there was little in the way of German opposition. After the completion of Operation Benedict, H.M.S. Argus once more returned to the Clyde for deck carrier duties. For training on the Firth of Clyde her usual position was off Arran and when flying on, the trainees had to catch one of six arrester wires. Each pilot had to complete six deck landings to qualify as a Fleet Air Arm pilot for carrier duties. During the autumn of 1941 she made more aircraft ferry voyages to Malta with H.M.S. Ark Royal, carrying Hurricanes, for re supply and Sea Hurricane fleet fighters for protection. But in the November operation, coded Perpetual, while she was approaching Gibraltar, H.M.S. Ark Royal was torpedoed and sunk. As the only operational aircraft carrier available to take her place, H.M.S. Argus joined Force H in the Mediterranean. On 7th March 1942 she covered H.M.S. Eagle on the first Spitfire resupply to Malta, in Operation Spotter, with all the aircraft landing safely. Once again with H.M.S. Eagle, she covered the convoy for Operation Harpoon in June and then carried the Fairey Fulmars of 807 Squadron and the Swordfish of 824 Squadron. In this operation she was part of Force T and her Fulmars shot down two enemy bombers, but her speed was a great source of concern. During July, Churchill suggested she be used for a special exercise in the Arctic. H.M.S. Argus was to accompany convoys protected by all the available warships and aircraft carriers and bulldoze the German opposition out of the way until the convoys reached Murmansk. Wisely the scheme went unnoticed at the Admiralty On the 31st July she joined H.M.S. Victorious as part of force M and exercised with four more carriers out in the Atlantic, as the prelude to the next operation. Operation Pedestal was the most important convoy re - supply operation to Malta during the war and the vessels sailed for the imperilled island in August. Though H.M.S. Argus was part of Force G she lay alongside at Gibraltar with spare aircraft, designated as a reserve carrier.

Argus with her bow strengthened

The Queen Bee radio controlled target

Swordfish goes into the barrier

Swordfish training aircraft

A Swordfish catches the wire

Argus with Force "H"

Argus with rebuilt bow

Hurricane resupply – Mediterranean	Hurricane resupply – Russia

Swordfish training aircraft at the bow	Seafires training for Operation "Torch"

Covering Spitfire supply for Malta	An aerial shot after "Harpoon"

Sea Hurricanes in the hangar

Sea Hurricane on finals

Fairey Fulmars

Hurricane at Takoradi

Exhaust smoke "Harpoon" Convoy

Swordfish lands during "Harpoon"

Seafire at Lamlash Scotland

Wildcats at Rothesay Bay, Bute

It had been felt that she was too vulnerable to air attack and it would only be a matter of time before she would be sunk. H.M.S. Furious, the other elderly carrier, was included in the Pedestal operation in a separate action. She was to carry Spitfires to Malta in Operation Bellows and it was during the Pedestal convoy that H.M.S. Eagle was sunk. During September 1942 Argus went to the Tyne for a refit and, by November 1942, she was back in the Western Mediterranean for the liberation of North Africa, Operation Torch.

As the oldest ship with the youngest crew, H.M.S. Argus was part of Force O, carrying the Seafire IIc of 880 Squadron from the aircraft carrier H.M.S. Indomitable. Her first duty was to protect the assault force, which had landed on 8th November. H.M.S. Argus was accompanied by the escort carrier H.M.S. Avenger for these actions. On one occasion a Fairey Albacore crash landed on her deck. The crew was rescued and the aeroplane was thrown over the side. She was also heavily targeted by submarines of the Vichy French. They consistently tried to torpedo her, but her draught and manoeuvrability saved her. Ten miles north of Algiers she was to sustain her first war damage when she was dive bombed by aeroplanes from Sicily. The bomb damage took out one of her four inch guns, killing the young crew and damaging some Seafires. This was followed by a series of near misses. Even though the after flight deck was damaged she still operated her Seafires.

The two carriers returned home from Gibraltar after the Torch operation, but on 15th November 1942 H.M.S. Avenger was torpedoed and sunk by the German submarine U 155. Only twelve of her crew were recovered. Avenger blew up and sank within two minutes, all within sight of H.M.S. Argus. The shortage of carriers at this stage in the war was now acute and she was quickly repaired on 22nd November at Elderslie Dock, Glasgow. December 1942 saw her as the senior officer's ship, escorting the North African troop convoy K.M.F. 5. She was back on the Clyde by the 31st December. Up to the end of February 1943 she had escorted two further troop convoys to Gibraltar and she was under repair until the end of April 1943. When she completed these repairs there was now a plentiful supply of aircraft carriers and she was clearly redundant for war service. Argus then reverted back to her status as deck landing training carrier on the

Clyde. For over a year she worked in the Firth of Clyde, flying and landing on and off a variety of aircraft. She was also used as a target for the "Highball" trials around November 1943. Highball was a smaller version of the Dambuster bomb, "Upkeep" and had been designed for anti-ship use, the main target being the German battleship Tirpitz. During the late summer of 1944 she was based at Rothesay Bay, operating the Fairey Swordfish and the Grumman Wildcats of 768 Training Squadron, Fleet Air Arm. One Wildcat crashed into her barrier, putting her out of service for twenty - four hours. Twenty six years after Bell - Davis took off from her deck a Fairey Swordfish took off from her flight deck in her last aeroplane take off. H.M.S. Argus was then placed into reserve with the Reserve Fleet at Chatham as a base and accommodation ship and was still carrying out this function when the war ended in Europe in May 1945. In the autumn of 1946 Argus was bought by the firm of T.W. Ward of Inverkeithing, Fife, for scrap. There was an outcry that she should be preserved because of her historical value, but by the end of 1947, H.M.S. Argus had been demolished for scrap.

(i)

BATTLE HONOURS

ATLANTIC	1941 – 42
ARCTIC	1941
MALTA CONVOYS	1942
NORTH AFRICA	1942

(ii)

Particulars of H.M.S. Argus [1924]

Length: 565' 11" **Breadth:** 68' 8" **Draught:** 21'
Displacement: 14450 tons **Fuel oil:** 2000 tons
Machinery: Four shaft turbines, S.H.P. 20000 = 21.21 knots
Armament: [2 x 4"] + [4 x 4"] + [4 x 3 pdrs.] + 10 Lewis m.g.
20 aeroplanes
Complement: 401 [1921 - 360, 1922 +1923 - 377]
Note: Laid down Dalmuir June 1914, purchased 1916 and launched 2 - 12 – 1917. Commissioned, Royal Navy: 14 - 9 - 1918. [War damage 1939 - 1945, 1 x 250 kg hit and several 1000 kg and 250 kg near misses]

(iii)

H.M.S. ARGUS
Attached Flights
1927 to 1930

Flight	Date	Aeroplane	Comments
401	May '28 to May '30	Flycatcher	China Station and Coastal Area, U.K
404	Mar '27 to May '28	Flycatcher	China Station, half flight Shanghai, full flight in March and June '27 only and January to May 1928
422	April '27 to June '29	Fairey IIId Blackburn	China Station and Coastal Area U.K.
441	Mar '27 to April '30	Fairey IIId Blackburn Fairey IIIf	China Station and Coastal Area U.K.
443	April '27 to April '27 May '28 to May '28	Fairey IIId	China Station half flight April '27
450	May '29 to May '30	Blackburn	Coastal Area U.K.

Note: Fleet Fighter 401 and 404 Flights Fleet Spotter 422 Flight
Fleet Reconnaissance 441, 443 and 450 Flight

(iv)

Deck Handling autumn 1944: 768 Training Squadron

Sunday 3rd September '44: 1019 Landed in 1 Wildcat-crashed into barrier, 1200 flying suspended, lack of wind. 1300 flew off 1 Wildcat, resumed DLCO training. 1525 flying completed: 4th, 5th, 7th and 8th all flying. 18th Sept: flying, Swordfish. ATC cadets on board overnight: 0927 – 1400hrs. 19th September, Swordfish flying, night flying commenced 2100. 20th September: Swordfish flying, flying completed 0212 – recommenced 1000. 21st September: night flying cancelled. 22nd September: flying completed 2250. 23rd September: flying abandoned 2200. 24th September: flying abandoned 2301

(v)

Brief post war description of H.M.S. Argus 1921

ARGUS (Emergency War Programme)

Begun by Beardmore as the Italian liner, "**Conte Rosso**" in 1914, she was purchased for the Navy in 1916, and completed as an aircraft carrier in 1918. In view of the difficulties experienced in landing on the deck of the " **Furious** " due to the air eddies caused by the hot furnace gases from the funnel and displacement currents from the upper-works, the " **Argus** " was designed with a perfectly clear flying deck from stem to stern and the furnace smoke and gases were expelled by fans through big horizontal smoke ducts opening out aft. Her chart house is raised and lowered on a lift and the two light wireless masts are hinged to fall flush with the deck. Twenty aeroplanes can be stowed in the hangar which is divided into four sections by fire-proof screens, and communicates with the flying deck by means of two lifts. Amidships are wind-breaking palisades which can be raised to protect machines on deck, and two derricks are fitted amidships and two cranes aft for lifting aircraft from the water. The hull contains large carpenters' and engineers' workshops, fully equipped for the maintenance and repair of aircraft; torpedoes and bombs for the aeroplanes are stored so that she is fitted in every way as a floating hangar and aerodrome, and as such has proved very successful.

Dimensions: 565 x 68 X 21 feet (mean) = 14,450 tons displacement.

Armament: Two 4-inch; four 4-inch A.A. No torpedo tubes.

Machinery: Turbines of 22,000 H.P. driving four screws = 20 knots.

Twelve boilers. Fuel: 2,000 tons oil.

Complement: 360 R.N. plus R.A.F.

Appearance: Differs from all the other carriers in having no funnels or mast.

(1921)

Commissioned Crew April 1944

In Command: Captain V. N. Surtees, DSO
Commander, (R.N.V.R.), J. M. Nairn (act.)
Lieut. - Com. G. Whitfield (ret.)
Lieut. - Com. H. M. Burrows (ret.)

Tempy. Lieut.-Com (**N***) C. E. Kirby (act)
Lieutenant (R.N.R.) M.E.R. Soper
Tempy. Lieut., (R.N.V.R.), A. H. B.Jones
Tempy. Lieut., (R.N.V.R.), H. J. Telfer
Tempy. Lieut., (R.N.V.R.), J. B. Selwyn
Tempy. Lieut (R.N.V.R.), K. G. Talbot-Scobie
Lieut.-Com. (**A**) (**P**) A. S. McTurk (act)
Lieutenant (**A**) (**P**) P. H. Chambers
Tempy. Lieut., (**A**) (R.N.V.R.), (**P**) N. G. Maclean
Tempy. Lieut., (**A**) (R.N.V.R.), J. J. Potter
Commander (**E**) (R.N.R.) W.W. Boosey
Lieutenant (**E**) W. Burton, M.B.E.
Lieutenant (**E**) R. K. Hows
Lieutenant (**E**) P. R. Marrack (act)
Tempy. Lieut., (**E**) L. E. Thomas
Tempy. Lieut., (**E**) R.N.Kinder
Captain, (R.M.) R. W. O'N. Collis (act)

Chaplain Rev. L. L. R. Griffiths, B.A. LTh
Paym.Com T. P. G. Bennett
Surg.Lieut.-Com. (R.N.V.R.), C. A. St. C. Hiley, M.R.C.S., L.R.C.P., (act.)
Tempy.Surg. Lieut (R.N.V.R.), C. D. Coe, M.B., chB
Paym. Lieut R. E. Williams
Paym.Lieut (R.N.V.R.), A. D.Taylor
Tempy. Paym.Lieut. (R.N.V.R.), B. Jackson
Tempy. Sub-Lieut., (R.N.V.R.), I. Mc.Innes
Tempy Sub-Lieut. (Sp.Br.), (R.N.V.R.), (Met.) G.W. Maskell
Gunner D. H. Rayment
Tempy. Gunner. (**T**) W. J. Pyle
Tempy Boatswain E- Stephenson (act)
Wt. Aircraft Offr. W. G. Carman
Wt. Aircraft Offr. (**0**) S.T.Jackson
Wt. Shipwright. . .J. G. Brownridge
Wt. Engineer H. K. Hosegood (act)
Schoolmaster N. J. Hague
Tempy. Wt. Elect. F.B.S.Bell (act)
Tempy. Wt. Supply Offr. R. Bray

768 Squadron
Tempy. Acting Sub-Lieut. (**A**), (R.N.V.R.), (**P**) K. Morley
Tempy. Acting Sub-Lieut. (**A**), (R.N.V.R.), (**O**) H.J Sendall
Tempy. Acting Sub-Lieut. (**A**), (R.N.Z.N.V.R.) (**P**) G. Y. Hooper

Beardmore School of Reserve Flying
Setting up the school
Aircraft at Renfrew
Some accidents, administration and closure

Before the outbreak of the Great War civilian flying schools which existed at such places as Brooklands and Liverpool were employed ultimately to train pilots for the Royal Flying Corps. When the war finished the idea of these schools was resurrected by the Royal Air Force which felt that the civilian flying schools would be an economic proposition in time of financial shortages. The schools were to be set up to retrain pilots who had seen service in the Great War and these pilots were to become members of the Reserve Air Force Officers (R. A. F. O.) In 1920 Lord Weir, the former Air Minister, was contacted by Lord Trenchard, the Chief of Air Staff, to find out his views on creating the R. A. F. O. and an Auxiliary or Territorial Air Force. Weir felt it was too soon after the war to create such organisations, since the war had been over barely two years and that there would be considerable recruitment problems. The plan was left to another Air Minister, Samuel Hoare, to take up and develop and in February 1922 plans were published.

In Scotland the idea was discussed at length by the Glasgow Branch of the Royal Aeronautical Society, of which William Beardmore and William Weir were members, but due to the prevailing economic circumstances brought about by a cut in government spending the plans were shelved for a year. The Air Ministry also felt that the Reserve Flying Schools would have an indirect and beneficial effect for the aircraft industry at a time of limited aircraft orders. They believed that R.A.F.O. members would also want to fly their own aircraft, giving the aircraft industry a double boost. This policy was clearly reflected in the Light Aeroplane Competitions of the 1920s when the Air Ministry wanted to find a cheap, reliable, dual control aeroplane to fill the demand they created. During February 1923 the Royal Air Force came to Glasgow and started to recruit members for the R. A. F. O. holding interviews at Taylor Street.

On 23rd July 1923 Beardmore set up the only flying school in Scotland, to train pilots for the R. A. F. O., at Renfrew Aerodrome.

Pilots from the North of England were included for the company to qualify for the treasury grant. To try and attract recruits for the new scheme and to keep the public aviation minded, the 1923 King's Cup Air Race was flown through Glasgow and the West of Scotland. (The winning trophy was presented by William Beardmore.) The race did not bring the flood of wanted recruits, even though it was enthusiastically followed by everyone at the time and for the Air Ministry came the problem of setting up other schools and running them.

During the war Renfrew had been set up as an Aircraft Acceptance Park by the Ministry of Munitions and was used to fly aeroplanes produced by the Clyde Shipyards in the Weir Scheme. The airfield was also designated as the base for a naval communications squadron or strike squadron and was used to store aircraft awaiting delivery to the air services. The Ministry of Munitions had completed the layout and construction of Renfrew and the handling of the building contracts became an investigation by the Select Committee on National Expenditure. Their investigation resulted in a court case and a not proven verdict against the contractors. The local post - war airfield plan meant that the airfield at Inchinnan was closed down, while the Air Ministry was to retain the land on which the old Beardmore airship factory stood, with the balance of the land being sold off. There were some post - war flights at Renfrew; on 10th April 1919 one aeroplane landed, later film was flown out to Gleneagles and four months later on 18th August 1919, the first commercial flight flew out. Between 1919 and 1922 flying at Renfrew was infrequent, due to the uncertainty of official thinking on aviation in Scotland.

Beardmore had flown some commercial operations with the W.B.IIb, but the Air Ministry was not really concerned or interested. The Ministry of Munitions tried to sell off the women's dormitory in 1921, but neither the Ministry's plans nor Beardmore's plans were a success. The Air Ministry had also given permission for members of the Scottish Branch of the Royal Aeronautical Society to use Renfrew's facilities, provided they paid for the petrol. This facility was well used by James Weir, brother of William Weir, who regularly flew in and out of Renfrew in his personal Boulton Paul aeroplane.

The evidence would seem to suggest that Beardmore were not happy at running the school and negotiations with the Air Ministry were long and protracted. It cost them £8288 to set up the school and even then it came under the authority of the Director General of Civil Aviation who in this case was Sir Sefton Brackner. He visited the school in June 1923 and left suitably impressed. (Brackner was one of the casualties of the R101 disaster, his body being identified by his monocle.) In its first two months of operation the school had about two dozen men under training, mostly from the West of Scotland, with its annual capacity being seventy pupils.

The Beardmore School was set up with aeroplanes that were similar to ones that were then in service with the Royal Air Force, such as the Avro 504, the DH 9 and the Bristol Fighter, the latter a Bristol 81 Puma Trainer. Each aircraft was painted with the company name, "William Beardmore & Co. Ltd.," and underneath, "Renfrew Flying School."

Avro 504 with students and instructors at Renfrew

DH 9 trainer G-EBIG

G-EBGZ with Kingwill and student

The refresher course was divided into two distinct phases, ground work and then actual flying. The School was managed from Dalmuir by A. J. Campbell, the location manager was R. C. Russell and the Chief Flying Instructor was Alan Kingwill, who had been a pilot with Berkshire Aviation. At Renfrew, Alan Kingwill had the use of an Avro 504, which he used to provide air experience to pilots before they joined the Beardmore School. Kingwill was regarded in contemporary publications as the founder of the Scottish Flying Club, with his business partner Mr "Red Hot" Jones, who was the club's chief flying instructor. The location manager at Renfrew, R.C. Russell, was originally in charge of the airship works at Inchinnan, but had moved to Renfrew when the works closed down. In addition to the Renfrew School, the Air Ministry had contracts with de Havilland, Bristol, Armstrong Siddeley Motors and North Sea Aerial and General Transport Limited.

1923 was not a good year for the schools; it was generally wet and windy, flying was infrequent and there was a great lack of recruits, but by the end of its first year of operation Renfrew had passed 74 recruits. 1924 involved the school in at least four crashes, which included the DH 9 crashing at Renfrew on the 30th October 1924. By June 1924 the Bristol Fighter had gone, having been leased from the Bristol Aeroplane Company Ltd. The most interesting crash of the year took place in December. While being flown by a Mr Michaelis, the Avro 504K, G – EBGZ, crashed into trees at Springburn Park. He had become completely disorientated in cloud and thought he was flying over the Trossachs. He lost his bearings and brought the 504 down in the trees near the statue of James Reid. This Avro 504 appeared to lead a charmed life; it survived the crash and continued in service until the school closed. That year, of the graduates, two became instructors at other schools, one became a pilot with Imperial Airways and one became a pilot in civil aviation.

To see that the school was being run along the correct lines it received periodic inspections from the Air Ministry. On 1st April 1925 Beardmore and the Air Ministry signed a four year contract, to provide further training at Renfrew. After three years training the school had flown 3857 hours covering a distance of 320000 miles with accidents being few and by May 1927 sixty- seven pilots had passed at the school for the year 1926 - 27. On 25th May 1927 a Bristol 89a Trainer, G-EBOD, crashed at Pollokshaws East Station. As the aircraft was flying over the south side of Glasgow it had engine failure over Plantation Quay. The pilot, Mr Fella, immediately thought of lighting a cigarette and trying to land. He believed he could reach Pollok Park and he headed in its direction, lost power and tried to land on the railway embankment. He hit a signal pole and the Bristol swung into the embankment and came to a halt. The machine was repaired and soon flying again.

   There were thirteen Bristol 89a trainers built between 1927 and 1931 for both the Renfrew and Bristol schools of reserve flying. Beardmore had built one Bristol 89a up from spares, after G-EBOD and G-EBQS had been repaired and found there was enough spare parts left to build another 89a Trainer. This was G-EBWN. The Bristols had started to replace the DH 9 from the end of May 1926, but the Avro 504 was still being used as the basic trainer. During May 1927 training was marred by the first fatal accident. Flying Officer Walker was killed when his aircraft stalled and spun into the ground, the aircraft destroyed. His body was taken to Renfrew police station mortuary.

   At that time a new training syllabus had been introduced when the supply of old aircrew from the Great War had all but dried up. The new pilots had to pass a medical examination before being allowed to fly the new course and then they had to pay a fee to Beardmore. The new course consisted of flying ten hours solo after initial instruction on the 504, qualifying the pilot for his "A" civil licence. He was then commissioned in the new Auxiliary Air Force and all his fees were refunded. Old pupils had to return each year for a refresher course. This involved the officer in a programme of thirty hours, with four hours flying and by the end of July 1928 Beardmore reported to the Air Ministry that the standard of the candidates was outstanding.

   Mr. Louden replaced Mr. Russell in 1928 as the location manager, but he now came under James Hamilton, Beardmore's works manager at Dalmuir. The assistant instructor was Mr. J. Houston who was once a Lovat Scout in the Great War. He had joined the R.F.C in 1918; by the time he was demobilised in December 1919 he was acting instructor at the School of Special Flying, Gosport. J. Houston was the son of George Houston, the Scottish artist. During 1928, due to government cutbacks, the number of flying days was cut, but there was an increase in flying hours for each pilot. This was to be an ominous sign for the school at Renfrew, for all was not well with the parent company, even though this side of the company operation was very profitable. Up to August 1928 the profit for the year at Renfrew was £13936: 1: 5 and the rental of the field was £320, with hangar rental at £1: 5: 0 a month. By the end of August 1928 all flying operations by William Beardmore & Co. Ltd. at Renfrew were stopped, but with residual income from the Air Ministry the profit from August to December was £4284: 9: 11. The company then paid off the instructors and kept one mechanic and a manager on the site, still renting the hangar from the Air Ministry. When the instructors left they gave two silver trophies to the Scottish Flying Club, to be presented as prizes from time to time.

Bristol Puma Trainer

An example of a Bristol 89 Trainer

G-EBQS a Bristol 89a over the Renfrewshire countryside

An example of a Bristol 89a

CLOSING OF RENFREW FLYING SCHOOL

The Air Ministry have decided to close down the Beardmore Flying School at Renfrew Aerodrome. This decision will take effect on Saturday, and it is feared that it will have a discouraging effect upon the progress of Scottish aviation generally, as the school has done much to foster interest in things connected with flying. The Beardmore Flying School was formed in 1923 with three permanent instructors, and during its five years of existence, a large number of fully qualified pilots have graduated through its medium. An average of 100 flying officers have yearly passed through the school and taken their place as competent pilots, but as the Air Ministry has concluded a contract to train officers for the Air Force Reserve and private work is not sufficient, the school naturally will be closed down for the meantime.

Renfrew Aerodrome will still be continued, however, as it is the headquarters of the City of Glasgow Bombing Squadron and the Scottish Flying Club. A considerable amount of constructional work remains to be carried through at the aviation department of the Beardmore Works at Dalmuir, and this will be unaffected by the Air Ministry's decision.

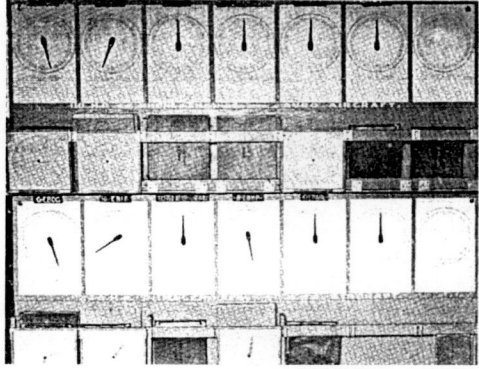

A newspaper report of closure   Aircraft maintenance clocks Renfrew

On the 16th October 1928 the board of directors was informed at Parkhead that the school had lost the contract to train pilots for the R.A.F.O. On 3rd November 1928 the school was closed permanently, with no flying taking place after that date. Five Bristol trainers, one Bristol 89, one DH 9 and one 504 were put up for sale on 19th December 1928 with the DH 9 and the 504 being sold on. The Bristols were broken up by a Renfrew scrap dealer, since no buyer could be found for them; they were just too expensive to run and insure. Alan Kingwill moved to Manchester at the end of November 1928 as manager of Northern Air Transport and he took with him the DH 9, G - EBIG. Northern Air Transport retained this DH 9 until December 1931 and it was reported as being on Islay with Kingwill on a proving flight in February 1929. James Hamilton moved to Handley Page aircraft and became involved with the designs of such aircraft as the Harrow and the Halifax and the development of the Handley Page slot. John Houston was killed in 1937 while flying a Percival Gull from Renfrew, over Johnston, Renfrewshire. The three other passengers were killed including M. O'B. S. Barrington, sales manager of the Percival Aircraft Company. The Avro 504, G-EBGZ, was bought by North British Aviation and was used by Captain Fresson for joy riding and pioneer flying in the Orkneys during September 1931.

On 28th January 1929 National Flying Services (N.F.S.) made an agreement with the Air Ministry to train pilots, the old training scheme being seen as too expensive to operate. By 22nd January 1931 six flying clubs were affiliated to N.F.S., with fourteen light aeroplane clubs approved for some form of financial assistance. William Beardmore & Co. Ltd., was not one of them.

School Aeroplanes

Avro 504K	G - EAHY	[H7513, Built by Hewlett & Blondeau 1918, Reg. 21. 9. 23, Canc. - 1. 29]
Avro 504K	G - EBCB	[H221, Built by Scottish Aviation 1918 - 1919, Reg. 16 . 3. 22 Canc. - 2. 29 used by Kingwill & Jones Flying Co. Based at Renfrew.]
Avro 504K	G - EBFV	[Dual Control. Reg. 30. 12. 23, Canc. 6. 10. 24. Built from spares, sold to W.B. by Berkshire Aviation.]
DH 9	G - EBGQ	[H5632. Built by Alliance Aeroplane Co. 1918 – 1919, Reg. 4. 6. 23, Canc. 30. 10. 24]
Avro 504K	G - EBGY	[LE 10390. Reg. 28. 6. 23, Canc. 12. 6. 24.]
Avro 504K	G - EBGZ	[LE 10407. Reg. 28. 6. 23., aerobatic, to North British Aviation. 7. 10. 29.]
DH 9	G - EBHP	[H9203. Built by Airco 1918 - 1919, Reg. 29. 8. 23, Canc. 18. 1. 26.]
DH 9C	G - EBIG	[H5886. Built by Alliance Aeroplane Co., 1918 – 1919 Reg. 25. 10. 23., to Northern Air Transport Ltd.18. 4. 29.]
Avro 504K	G - EBIS	[R/LE/12663. Reg. 29. 2. 24., to North British Aviation 27. 2. 29.]
Bristol 89	G - EBNZ	[6963. Reg. 26. 4. 26 sold unknown fate 14. 1. 30.]
Bristol 89	G - EBOA	[6964. Reg. 26. 4. 26 Canc. 15. 3. 27]
Bristol 89a	G - EBOD	[6966. Reg. 13. 4. 27 Canc. 14. 1. 30]
Bristol 89a	G - EBQS	[6967. Reg. 24. 6. 27. Canc. 14. 1. 30]
Bristol 89a	G - EBWN	[R58. Built from spares, Reg. 1. 3. 28. Can. 14. 1. 30]

Note:- The other school machines were, **G - EBXA [AVRO 504K], G – EBSB, G -EBVR [Bristol 89a] and G - EBDG [DH 9]**

The leased Puma engined Bristol Fighter has proved impossible to trace accurately, but we do know that the aircraft was a Type 81 Puma Trainer. The first Type 81 was a conversion of a Type 29 tourer (**G-EAXA**). This aircraft had its registration cancelled at the same time as the leased aircraft was returned to Filton from Renfrew on May the 10th 1924, the lease expiring in June. The balance of probability is on the side of **G-EAXA** being the aircraft at Renfrew. The four other Type 81 Puma Trainers were **G-EBFR** C/N 6239, **G-EBFS** C/N 6240, **G-EBFT** C/N 6241, and **G-EBFU** C/N 6242. The last two had oleo undercarriages.

(The list compiled with the assistance of the C.A.A.)

Appendices

A. Beardmore Farquhar Machine Gun   Page 218

B. Rohrbach Aircraft   Page 220

C. Aircraft Armament and Ammunition   Page 223

D. Scottish Aircraft Production   Page 225

E. Aircraft Orders Ministry of Munitions   Page 227

F. Arrol Johnston   Page 228

G. Output of Aeroplanes   Page 230

H. Output of Aero-Engines   Page 231

I. Aircraft manufactured for or at Dalmuir   Page 232

J. Airframe manufacturers connected with Dalmuir   Page 234

K. Bibliography   Page 235

APPENDIX A
Beardmore - Farquhar Machine Gun

In 1915 the Admiralty adopted the .303 Farquhar - Hill automatic rifle for naval service use, aboard establishments and ships. In 1917 this rifle went through a series of War Office trials, but was rejected. Later on an order for twenty rifles was placed by the War Office for more investigations and experiments. In 1918 the feasibility of introducing this automatic rifle into the army was once again studied and from this study came a follow on order for another twenty rifles.

In May 1918 the Ministry of Munitions placed an order for one hundred thousand of these rifles with Messrs Farquhar – Hill, with the components to be made at the Standard Small Arms Factory. The stocks and barrels were to be made at National Rifle Factory No. 2 and the whole weapon was to be assembled at the Training School of Birmingham .In July 1918 the War Office reconsidered the rifle supply situation, such as reconditioning and repairing, the possibility of a rifle shortage due to wastage in the field and the time taken to train the troops with the new rifle, for the 1919 spring campaign. By October 1918 the battlefield situation was in favour of the Allies, the rifle programme was settled by the army, the Farquhar - Hill Rifle was cancelled and the designated factories closed. With no prospect of his rifle being adopted by the army or the navy, Colonel M.G. Farquhar redesigned the rifle into a light, drum fed, machine - gun for infantry and aircraft use. It was test flown in a Bristol Fighter during November 1919. One gun was fitted to a Scarf ring on the Fighter for use by the observer, but with his final shot the gun jammed. The feeling from the authorities was that the gun was not good enough. Though it was a failure, this gun attracted the attention of the Admiralty, who wanted Beardmore to manufacture it at Parkhead. It had a weight of sixteen and a quarter pounds, a rate of fire of 480 rounds per minute and it used a 77 round, .303 magazine. The post-war machine guns were manufactured at the premises of Webley and Scott in Birmingham, from 1919 to July 1922, then from August 1922 to December 1922 at F.E. Baker, the motorcycle firm, a subsidiary of Beardmore. The machine guns were regularly tested by the Experimental Officer at Hythe, who reported the result of the trials to the War Office Small Arms Committee. In these reports he felt that the claims of the manufacturer, such as never jamming or parts never breaking, were unjustifiable and that the tests were a waste of ammunition. Though three were installed in the Beardmore Latvian fighter, the only variant of the gun, which arose any interest from the military was a .5 inch version, with one being submitted for test. The result was the same; none was ordered for the armed forces. In 1928 Parkhead recorded a loss of £20000 on the production of the Beardmore - Farquhar Machine Guns, which were then in store at F.E. Baker. As a director of Webley and Scott, Colonel Farquhar continued the weapons development into a 1934 model, but it still wasn't good enough for the armed forces and not one was ordered. By then the Beardmore involvement was in name only.

Short Specification

Calibre: 0.303 Feed: 77 round drum magazine Weight: 16 ¼ lbs.
Operation: Gas and spring actuated   Type of lock: Rotating bolt head

The Beardmore Farquhar Machine Gun for infantry use

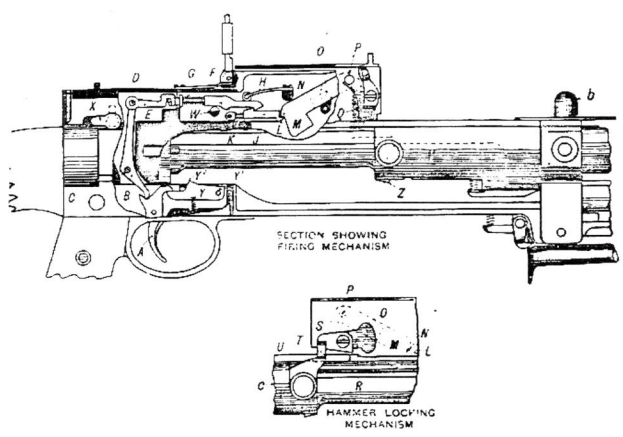

The firing mechanism

APPENDIX B
Rohrbach Aircraft

Adolf Karl Rohrbach was born in Gotha, the son of a headmaster. He served his apprenticeship with the shipbuilders Blohm and Voss and during the Great War he worked with Claude Dornier at the Friedrichshafen Airship Works. Ultimately he became the chief designer of Zeppelin, working on giant bombers. The terms of the Versailles Treaty meant that all aeroplane manufacture was stopped in Germany. The Giant Zeppelin, all metal, four engined, R4/20, that he was working on was scrapped on the 21st November 1922. In 1922 Adolf K. Rohrbach founded Rohrbach Metal Flugzeugbau in Berlin. Though most of the Rohrbach aircraft were assembled in Denmark from German parts supplied from Berlin, Beardmore manufactured many wing and fuselage components. The Rohrbach aeroplane was built almost entirely of the metal duralumin. It had a thick wing section and a box centre section with thinner leading and trailing edges. They were all monoplanes and the flying boats used two large side floats, close to the fuselage, on a flat sided hull with two or three steps. In 1923 Rohrbach produce the RO II, powered by two Rolls - Royce Eagles. Ten of this version was bought by Japan as the Mitsubishi R Type. From this design stemmed the RO III, which was produced in 1924. The Rodra, a development of the RO III, was powered by Lorraine Dietrech engines and two were supplied to Turkey. They were named, "Istanbul" and "Izmir." They had a top speed of 122 miles per hour, a service ceiling of 11000 feet, with the engines developing a total of 900 H.P. During 1926 a further flying boat was developed for training and experimental work. This was called the Robbe I and was followed in 1927 by the Robbe II, with its engines mounted above the wing as pushers. In 1926 the company had departed from its design philosophy of only producing flying boats and transports, by producing a fighter for Turkey. It was a small single engined, single seat monoplane with a high wing, but it never progressed from the prototype stage, both crashing and, on one flight killing, the test pilot. They also investigated an aircraft with rotating wings.

The Rocco of 1927 differed from all the other designs in having tapered wings which had been pioneered by the Robbe II. The Rocco had a crew of three and accommodation for ten passengers. This aircraft was powered by Rolls - Royce Condors, with the fuel tanks in the wing and having a maximum speed of 125 miles per hour. The next Rohrbach design was the Romar of 1928, which was powered by three over wing B.M.W. geared engines driving four bladed propellers. The tapered wings had a span of one hundred and twenty one feet with a maximum chord of twenty six feet three inches at the root, which was three feet deep. The underside sloped up to the wing tips, measuring eight feet two inches. The second Romar was built in April 1929 and created a world altitude record of, 7218 feet with a payload of six and a half tons. In total there were four Romars built. The Robbe was developed in 1928 for long distance and passenger freight and was powered by two Gnome - Jupiter or two Pratt & Whitney Hornets. The most successful Rohrbach design was the twenty seat Roland airliner, which was built for Lufthansa. The Roland of 1928 was not a flying boat, but a landplane and was first used to provide a scheduled service from Munich to Milan. The Roland had twenty two world records to its credit, all gained when flown by Hermann Steindorf, the company test pilot. Latterly the Roland could be seen at Croydon Aerodrome, London or in Spain, sharing all the Lufthansa services with the J.U. 52. The Roland was one of the first airliners with a totally enclosed cockpit. In all Rohrbach produced twelve aircraft types, of which about fifty were built.

Ro II on makers trials

The Rodra under construction

The Japanese Rohrbach

Rohrbach Ro II commencing trials

The Turkish Rohrbach

The Rohrbach Rofix

The Romar flying boat

The first modern airliner the Roland

Roland comes into land

The early Roland open cockpit

The Rohrbach Rocco on trials

The Rohrbach Rocco at Kopenhagen

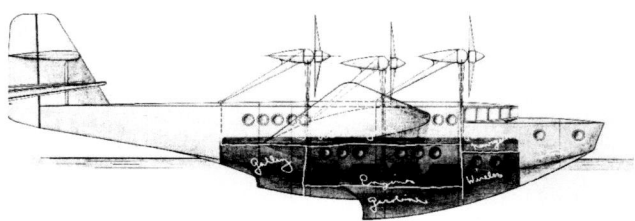
The Rohrbach Rolantic four engined projected flying boat

APPENDIX C

Aircraft Armament and Ammunition

The Vickers .303 machine gun, was the standard pilot's gun of the Great War, having an interrupter gear, either Constantinescu, Kauper etc., for firing through the propeller. A converted ground gun, it was changed from water cooling to air cooling by perforating the cooling case around the barrel. It was belt fed, but the original cloth strip caused jamming due to dampness and was replaced with a disintegrating belt copied from the Germans. The Vickers .303 machine gun was only approved for air use in 1917. In addition to Vickers manufacturing the gun at Crayford and Erith, orders were placed with the Colt Company of America. To increase the rate of fire a Hazelton speed up device was fitted as a nose cap which increased the rate of fire to about a thousand rounds per minute.

The Admiralty received all its aircraft ammunition from War Office stocks and the regular allotment for the R.N.A.S. was fifty thousand rounds of S.P.G. (tracer) ammunition per demand. The Admiralty replaced the Le Prieur rocket apparatus with Buckingham and P.S.A. incendiary rounds for anti - airship work from War Office stocks. The introduction of interrupter gear with the Vickers machine gun meant that all the .303 rounds had to be weighed, tested and centred with most of the attention being directed at the firing caps. This attention to the ammunition resulted in the near elimination of misfires, jams and shot airscrews.

The other aircraft machine gun was the Lewis gun. First adopted because of its lightness, the .303, Lewis machine gun became the standard aircraft observer's gun. Originally from America, it was found unsuitable for use with an interrupter gear and on aeroplanes the outer cylindrical cooling casing was removed and the gun used with a bare barrel. It was first ordered in 1913 and again in July 1914 and was fed with a top round magazine of 47 or 97 rounds, the gun being manufactured in Britain by the Birmingham Small Arms Company (B.S.A.). The Lewis gun lasted throughout the Great War with many examples being used in the Second World War. The most favoured combination in an ammunition belt or drum was a five round ratio of Buckingham, armour piercing, one S.A.A. round, armour piercing round and finally one S.A.A. round.

On aircraft, the Vickers aircraft gun and its derivatives lasted into the nineteen thirties and were replaced by the American Colt – Browning, but many examples of the ground gun were still in use in the nineteen sixties.

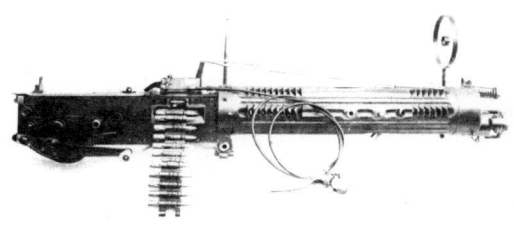

The Vickers machine gun modified for aircraft use

A Lewis gun stripped for instruction

Metal linked ammunition belt

Lewis and Vickers guns required from June 1918 to June 1919
(Ministry of Munitions table)

	British	Allies	Total
Vickers	34970	7200	42170
Lewis	20020	6000	26020

Note: From September 1918 demand was increased and met by 600 Lewis and 700 Vickers monthly.

APPENDIX D

Scottish Aircraft Production in the West of Scotland during the Great War

On the 7th January 1915 A.P. Henderson of the Partick shipbuilders D. & W. Henderson and brother of David Henderson, head of the R.F.C., contacted William Weir with a view to producing aeroplanes in the West of Scotland. The initial contract was to be two to four hundred aeroplanes and the work was to be completed by members of the local Engineer Employers Association, on a subcontract basis from Weir. The members of the group were Napier & Miller at Old Kilpatrick, Denny at Dumbarton, Stephens of Linthouse, and Barclay Curle at Whiteinch, The North British Locomotive Company, Springburn and Weir at Cathcart. The first Stephens of Linthouse machine flew at Renfrew on 20th August 1915 and was a B.E 2c. The North British Locomotive company assembled only fifty B.E 2cs leaving the scheme to concentrate on heavy engineering, such as tanks.

   The Weir scheme became a model of its kind and was adopted throughout the country. Nowadays the supply system of aircraft parts to the manufacturer would be called, "Just in time." The scheme relied heavily on sub - contract work with such people as woodworkers, carpenters, coffin makers and furniture makers, such as H. Morris & Co. Ltd and Wylie and Lochead. The greatest triumph was the introduction of women workers assembling and fitting out the aeroplanes. The first member of the group to encourage women was Napier & Miller at Old Kilpatrick in August 1915. In addition to the B.E 2c, the group produced the B.E. 2e, the F.E.2b and the Airco DH 9. Of the 4390 aeroplanes produced, the highest output was achieved during October 1918, when 292 aeroplanes were manufactured.

   At the war's end there were eleven firms producing twelve aircraft types, with one hundred and ten sub-contractors, including Singer at Clydebank. At Clydebank, Singer produced, in addition to service rifles, aircraft undercarriages, aeroplane fuselages and even the aeroplane nuts and bolts. Beardmore were deliberately kept out the scheme, since they were Admiralty contractors. The Fairfield Engineering Company also produced the Sopwith Cuckoo for the Admiralty. Their contract for one hundred aeroplanes was dated 16th October 1917 and their first aeroplane, N7001, flew at Renfrew on 25th July 1918. New aeroplane manufacturing was stopped at the end of December 1918, with the contracts being liquidated and the aeroplanes being broken up on the stocks, though some types were completed in 1919.

Totals

1915	237	**1917**	1234
1916	556	**1918**	2363

There follows a list of surviving aircraft contracts placed from 1916. The company name in brackets means that the contract was sub-contracted from Weir. If it is divided by a line it means the contract was a joint order with Weir.

Selection of some West of Scotland aircraft contracts

1. BE2e:- Weir   AS7357   Total   350, delivered 20 by Dec. 1917 Sub-contract to Barclay Curle (6 del. by Dec) Denny (7 del. by Dec)
2. BE2e:- Weir (Barclay Curle) 87a601 Total 50. 39 delivered by June 1917
3. BE2e:- Weir (Denny) N/D Total 50. 36 delivered by June 1917
4. BE2e:- Weir (Napier) N/D Total 50. 26 delivered by June 1917
5. FE2b:- Weir/Stephens 94A210 Total 300. 12 delivered by Dec. 1916
6. FE2b:- Weir/Stephens 87A1283 Total 300. 95 delivered by June 1917
7. DH9:- Weir AS14570 Total 300. 170 delivered by June 1918
8. DH9:- Weir AS41634 Total 300.
9. BE2e:-Weir AS7357 Total 350. 21 delivered by Dec 1917
10. BE2e:-Barclay Curle/Denny/Napier/British Caudron AS15178 Total 350.
11. FE2b:- Weir (Stephens/Barclay Curle) AS40817 Total 150. 54 delivered by June 1918.
12. FE2b:- Barclay Curle 35a/3047/c3518 Total 50. Cancelled 26/10/ 1918.
13. FE2b:- Weir (Barclay Curle) 35a/1076/C908 or 35a/1077/C907 Total 50 (42 cancelled 25/1/1919) 4 delivered Dec 1918 and 4 May 1919.
14. DH9:- Weir AS41634 Total 100. 85 delivered by Dec. 1918. Balance cancelled under War Break Clause.
15. DH9:- Weir 35a/2336/C2643 Total 50. Contract cancelled under War Break Clause.
16. Sopwith Cuckoo: - Fairfield, Govan AS.27863 Total 100. Fifty cancelled January 1919.

Women making BE2c wings

A revolution at work

APPENDIX E
Aircraft Orders Ministry of Munitions

On order 1 March 1917
Government Design

B.E 2c and d	51
B.E. 2e	733
B.E. 12	4
F.E. 8	19
F.E. 9	27
F.E. 2b	483
R.E. 8	1257
S.E. 5	474

Private Design

A.W.F.K. 3	74
A.W.F.K. 8	206
Avro 504 A and J	434
Avro 179	65
Avro 504c	50
Bristol Scout	6
Bristol Fighter	558
Caudron	13
Curtiss J.N 4	200
D.H 1	38
D.H. 2	33
D.H. 4	1009
D.H. 5	450
D.H. 6	220
M.Farman S.H	862
M. Farman L.H.	71

On order 1 March 1918
All designs

B.E. 2e	268
F.E. 9	7
F.E. 2b	510
R.E. 8	1681
S.E. 5	2928
A.W.F.K. 3	17
A.W.F.K. 8	432
Avro	4171
Bristol fighter	2892
D.H. 4	121
D.H. 6	822
D.H 9	3631
Handley Page	544
Martinsyde S/str	150
Sopwith Pup	394
Sopwith Camel	2199
Sopwith Dolphin	1571
Spad	95

Aircraft on order 1 March 1917 (Continued)

H. Farman	169	Camel	50
Handley Page	24	Triplane	101
Martinsyde S/seater	71	Bomber	200
110 H.P. Morane	33	Spad	256
Nieuport	130	Vickers F.B. 9	74
Sopwith 2/Seater	397	Vickers F.B. 12c	52
Pup	815	Vickers F.B. 14	90

Members of 148th Aero Squadron, starting on a daylight D.H.9 raid, at Petite Synthe, France Aug. 6th, 1918. L to R, Lieut. Morton Newhall, C.O. of squadron, Lieut. E.O. Harre in coat, pilot Maj. S.S. Hales (R.A.F.), Cpl. Edward Schneider, film cameraman. Note the compactness of the cockpit and armament on the group built D.H.9.

APPENDIX F

Arrol Johnston Ltd.

In 1902 William Beardmore became the majority shareholder in the fledgling Scottish car firm of Arrol Johnston at Paisley. When the Beardmore Company moved into the aero - engine business, just before the war, it was decided that aero- engines should be produced at the Heathhall works of Arrol Johnston, at Dumfries. William Beardmore had moved car manufacturing from Paisley, in order to be closer to the English market. The Heathhall factory was officially opened on 29th July 1913 under the management of T.C. Pullinger. By early 1914 Arrol Johnston had completed two 120 H.P. Beardmore Austro – Daimler aero-engines and had submitted them to the War Office for the aero engine competition that year.

When war broke out Arrol Johnston still retained its Paisley factory and this was purchased by William Beardmore & Co., Ltd., for the production of shells. At Heathhall, wartime manufacturing centred on three production lines, one for machine gun mounts, one for the manufacture of aeroplane wings and tails and the most important one for the manufacture of aero engines. With the phasing out of the six cylinder Austro - Daimler series there was spare capacity and Beardmore sub - contracted the assembly of Sopwith 2F-1 Camels from Dalmuir to the works. For the manufacture of aero - engines and other wartime activities Arrol Johnston employed about 2000 employees, most of them women.

After the war the company went back into the motor car business, still being managed by Pullinger. After the war his daughter, Dorothea returned from Vickers at Barrow, to run the canteen as deputy manager of the works. Earlier she had converted the Austro Daimler aero engine designs from metric to imperial measurements for her father. During the nineteen twenties the company worked closely with the Aster Motor Car Company and went on to produce the Arrol Aster luxury motor car. It was powered by a sleeve valve engine which used the Burt – McCollum system that had been used in the earlier Argyll car. It was this system which was adapted by Bristol Aero Engines in their radial engines, including the Bristol Hercules series. There was also one version of the Arrol Aster car built with a supercharger. Up to the time of its closure, Arrol Johnston was still wholly owned by William Beardmore, who liquidated the company in 1929.

Dorothea Pullinger

Arrol-Aster sleeve valve

APPENDIX G

Output of Aeroplanes August 1914 to December 1918

	1914	1915	1916	1917	1918	Total
Aeroplanes						
Single seater						
Home	20	224	706	4462	11481	17083
Abroad	0	67	173	587	39	866
Two - seater						
Home	103	1423	4953	9037	18721	34237
Abroad	4	580	737	467	70	2858
Experimental						
Home	60	34	46	57	72	269
Abroad	3	14	7	12	2	38
Twin engined bomber	0	0	11	30	391	432
Four engined bomber	0	0	0	0	6	6
Total						
Home	193	1681	5716	13766	30671	52027
Abroad	7	661	917	1066	111	2762
Grand Total	200	2342	6633	14832	30782	54789
Seaplanes and Ship aeroplanes						
Home	52	250	430	910	936	2578
Abroad	0	12	0	0	2	14
Total	52	262	430	910	938	2592
Boat Seaplanes						
Home	0	2	3	72	411	488
Abroad	4	75	21	75	100	275
Total	4	77	24	147	511	763

Note: Includes those actually handed to service

APPENDIX H

Output of Aero Engines August 1914 to December 1918

	1914	1915	1916	1917	1918	Total
Stationary Water Cooled						
Home	51	545	1500	4945	11630	18671
Abroad	4	111	322	2344	6530	9311
Total	55	656	1822	7289	18160	27982
Stationary Air - Cooled						
Home	13	820	2339	3288	2926	9396
Abroad	16	221	630	198	159	1124
Total	29	1041	2969	3486	2955	10520
Rotary						
Home	31	350	1500	3504	7508	12893
Abroad	15	567	912	2326	2582	6402
Total	46	917	2412	5830	10090	19295
Experimental						
Home	4	6	24	26	14	74
Abroad	4	12	0	34	10	60
Total	8	18	24	60	24	134
Total						
Home	99	1721	5363	11763	22088	41034
Abroad	39	911	1864	4902	9181	16897
Grand Total	138	2632	7227	16665	31269	57931

Note: Includes engines handed over for service.

APPENDIX I

Aircraft manufactured for or by
William Beardmore & Co., Ltd., Dalmuir

Beardmore Contract No.	Type	Serial No.	Total
	D.F.W	154	1
	D.F.W Military	891	1
	Seaplane [1914]		1 [Not Completed]
524	B.E 2c	1099 - 1122	24 + 12 fuselages
532	Wight 840	1400 - 1411	12
	Sopwith Pup		30 [Not traced]
539	Wight 840	9021 - 9040	24 [4 not traced]
541	B.E 2c	8326 - 8337	86 [50 not traced]
		8488 - 8500	
		8714 - 8724	
552	Nieuport XII	9201 - 9250	
		A5183 - A5202	70
562	Sopwith Pup	9901 - 9950	50
576	Sopwith Pup	N6430 - N6459	30
579	S.B.3d	N6100 - N6129	
		N6680 - N6749	100
598	Sopwith 2F-1	N6750 - N6849	
		N7100 - N7139	140
601	V/1500	E8287 - E8306	20 (Seven delivered)
		F8201 - F8230	30 (None delivered)
609	Sopwith 2F-1	N7650 - N7679	30 (Possibly Arrol Johnston took over contract)

1097	Experimental Bomb Dropper [W.B.1.]	B9467/N525	1
1110	Experimental Gun Carriage Machine		1(Not completed)
1133	W.B. II	F2995	1
1264/65/66	W.B. IV & V	N38, N41, N42	3 [N1a type]
1267	W.B. VII	Aircraft Ship Scout	1 (Not completed)
5306	W.B.VIa		1 (Not completed)
5404	W.B. IX	G - EAQI	1 (Not completed)
5422	W.B. X	G -EAQJ	1
5441/1	W.B. IIb	G - EARX & G - EARY	2
AV 1	Beardmore Inflexible	J7557/G-EBNG	1
AV 2	W.B. XXIV [Wee Bee]	G - EBJJ	1
AV 3	W.B. XXVI [Latvian Fighter]		1
AV 5	Beardmore Inverness	N183/N184	2

AIRSHIPS

Beardmore Contract No	Type	Details
1277	Spherical Balloons	No details available
1145	Kite Balloons	Four manufactured
545	No. 24	One built, scrapped December 1919
553	No. 27	One, destroyed by fire August 1919
554	No 28	One, cancelled 1917
575	R34	One, dismantled after crash January 1921
578	R36	G – FAAF, Scrapped
614	R40	Cancelled

.

APPENDIX J

Airframe manufacturers connected with Dalmuir

[Through manufacture aero - engine, design teams or agreement]

DALMUIR

SHORT NIEUPORT WIGHT SOPWITH

VICKERS

HANDLEY PAGE HAWKER AVRO

ARMSTRONG - WHITWORTH ROHRBACH

WESER

FOCKE- WULF BOEING DOUGLAS

NORTHROP DE HAVILLAND MONO SPAR

GENERAL AIRCRAFT

BLACKBURN V.F.W HAWKER SIDDELEY

BRITISH AIRCRAFT CORPORATION

M.B.B. BRITISH AEROSPACE

APPENDIX K
BIBLIOGRAPHY
Newspapers and periodicals

Aero, Aero Modeller, Aeroplane, Air Enthusiast, Aircraft Illustrated, Aircraft Illustrated Extra, Air International, Air Pictorial, The Baillie, Beardmore News, The Bulletin, The Daily Record, Engineer, Engineering, Fleet Air Arm Review, Flight, The Glasgow Herald, Motor, Royal Air Force Flying Review, Scale Model Aircraft, The Scots Magazine, Ship's Monthly, Syren & Shipping, Surplus, The Times.

Parliamentary and Government Papers

Report on the Royal Aircraft Factory, Treaties on Flax, The Airship Contract, The Air Estimates 1919 - 1932, Memorandum on Naval and Military Aviation 1912 and 1913, Proceedings of the Second Air Conference, Report of the British Cellulose Enquiry Committee, Report on the loss of the R101, Appropriation Accounts of the Ministry of Munitions, Reports on the Select Committee on National Expenditure, Supplements to the London Gazette 1915 to 1919, Return of Shipping Casualties and Loss of Life, Advisory Committee on Aeronautics Annual Reports, Final Report on the Administration and Command of the R.F.C., British Air Effort during the War, Cmd100, Report of the War Cabinet Committee on Women in Industry, Cmd 135, Reports of the Select Committee on Public Accounts 1916 to 1919.

[Source for the above - The Index to Parliamentary Papers 1900 to 1949 the Mitchell Library Glasgow]

Select Bibliography

Airfix.	Aircraft Modelling Guide 2, London, Airfix, 1974
Attard, J.	Britain and Malta, ----, P.E.G. Ltd., 1988.
Balfour, H.	Wings over Westminster, London, Hutchison, 1973
Banks, F.R.	I Kept no Diary, London, Airlife, 1978
Barnes, C.H.	Bristol Aircraft since 1910, London, Putnam, 1970
Birkenhead, Earl of	The Prof in Two World Wars, London, Collins, 1961.
Botting, D.	The Giant Airships, Alexandria Va., Time - Life Books, 1980.
Bowman, G.	War In The Air, London, Pan, 1958.
Bowyer, Chaz.	Hurricane at War, London, Ian Allen, n.d British Military Aircraft, Bison, 1982.
British Aerospace	75 years of Aviation at Kingston, British Aerospace, 1987
Brooks, P.W.	The Modern Airliner, London, Putnam, 1961.

Brown, J.D.	Carrier Operations in W.W. 2, Volume 1, London, Ian Allen, 1969.
Bruce, J.M.	British Aeroplanes 1914 - 18, London, Putnam, 1957. Warplanes of the First World War, Volumes One, Two and Three, London, McDonald, 1968.
Casey, L.S.	The illustrated History of Seaplanes and Flying Boats, London, Hamlyn, 1980.
Batchelor, J.	Naval Aircraft 1914 - 39, London, Phoebus, 1976.
Churchill, W.S.	The World Crisis, 1911 - 1918, London, Macmillan, 1942
	The Second World War, London, Cassel, 1948.
Cole, C.	McCudden V.C., London, Kimber, 1967.
Collier, C.	The Airship a History, London, Hart - Davis, Mac Gibbon, 1974.
Edwards, K.	The Navy of Today, London and Glasgow, Blackie, 1943.
Fresson, E.E.	Air Road to the Isles, London, Rendel, 1967.
Gallacher, W.	Revolt on the Clyde, London, Lawrence and Wishart, 1936.
Gibbs - Smith, C.H.	The Aeroplane, London, Science Museum, 1960.
Gillies, J.D. & Wood, J.L.	Aviation in Scotland, Glasgow, Royal Aeronautical Society, 1966.
Golley, J	Hurricanes over Murmansk, Wellingborough, Patrick Stephens, 1987.
Goodal, M.	The Wight Aircraft, London, Gentry Books, 1973.
Gresham Publishing Company	The Great World War, London, Gresham, 1914 to 1919.
Hanson, N.	Carrier Pilot, London, Futura, 1980.
Harvie, C.	No Gods and Precious Few Heroes, Scotland 1914 to 1980. London, Arnold, 1981.
Higham, R.	The British Rigid Airship, London, Foulis, 1961.
Hood, J. [Ed.]	The History of Clydebank, Clydebank District Council, 1988.
Hume, J.R. & Moss, M.S.	Beardmore, The History of a Scottish Industrial Giant London, Heinemann, 1979.
C.G.Grey [Ed.]	All the World's Aircraft, 1912 to 1931, London, Janes all World's Ships n.d
Jones, H.A. & Raleigh, W.	The War in the Air, Oxford, Clarendon Press, 1922 to 1937.

Joubert, P.B.	The Fated Sky, London, Hutchison, 1952
	The Third Service, London, Thames Dutton, 1955.
Kilbarchan, Lord,	Bring Back My Stringbag, London, Pan, 1979.
King, H.F.	Sopwith Aircraft, 1912 to 1920, London, Putnam, 1981.
Kinsey, G.	Martlesham Heath, Lavenham, Dalton, 1975.
Kirkwood, D.	My Life of Revolt, London, Harrap, 1935.
H.M. Le Fleming.	Warships of World War One, London, Ian Allen, 1967.
Lee, D.	Never stop the engine when it's hot, London, Thomas Harmsworth,1983.
Lenton, H.T. & Colledge, J.J.	Warships of World War Two, London, Ian Allen, 1967.
Lewis, C.S.	Sagittarius Rising, Harmondsworth, Penguin, 1977.
Liddel - Hart, B.	War Memoirs of David Lloyd George, London, Odhams, 1938.
McKee, A.	The Friendless Sky, London, New English Library, 1972.
McKinty, A.	Father of British Airships, London, Kimber, 1972.
Munson, K.	Aircraft of World War One, London, Ian Allen, 1967.
Naish, G.P.B.	Flying in the Royal Navy 1914 - 1964, H.M.S.O., London, 1964
Penrose, H.	British Aviation the Adventuring Years [1920 - 29], London, Putnam, 1973.
Polmar, N.	Aircraft Carriers, London, McDonald, 1970.
Poolman, K.	Scourge of the Atlantic, London, Book Club Associates, 1979
	Faith, Hope and Charity, London, New English, Library, 1974.
Popham, H.	Into Wind, London, Hamish Hamilton, 1969
	Sea Flight, London, Futura, 1974.
Reader, W.J.	Architect of Air Power, London, Collins, 1968.
	The Weir Group, A Centenary History, Glasgow, Weir, 1971.
Reynolds, Q.	They Fought for The Sky, London, Pan, 1974.
Robertson, B.	Sopwith, The man and his aircraft, London, Harleyford, 1971.
	British Military Aircraft Serials 1912 – 1978, Cambridge, Patrick Stephens, 1978
Scott, W.R. & Cunnison, J.	The Industries of the Clyde during the War, Oxford Clarendon, 1927.

Shores, C. & Cull, B.	Malta The Hurricane Years, London, Grub Street, 1987.
Shute, N.	Slide Rule, London, Heinemann, 1956.
Sprigg, C.	Great Flights, London, Nelson, 1936.
Sumner, P.H.	Marine Aircraft, London, Crosby Lockwood & Co., 1929
Thomas, M.	Out on a Wing, London, Michael Joseph, 1964.
Thorratt, G.	Aircraft Production Illustration, New York, McGraw – Hill, 1944.
Walker, P.	Early Aviation at Farnborough, Vol. One and Two, London, McDonald, 1971 and 1974.
Waverly.	The History of the Great War, London, Waverly, 1919.
Winton, J.	Find Fix and Strike, London, Batsford, 1980.
Wragg, D.	Wings over the Sea, London, David and Charles, 1979.
Yates, L.K.	The Women's Part in the War, London, Hodder and Stoughton, 1918.